WHIMSICAL TREATS

REINDEER FOOD

85 FESTIVE SWEETS AND TREATS TO MAKE A MAGICAL CHRISTMAS

CAYLA GALLAGHER

Skyhorse Publishing

Visit our website at www.skyhorsepublishing.com.

10 9 8 7 6 5 4 3 2 1

Library of Congress Cataloging-in-Publication Data

Names: Gallagher, Cayla, author.
Title: Reindeer food: 85 festive sweets and treats to make a magical
  Christmas / Cayla Gallagher.
New York, NY: Skyhorse Publishing, 2020. | Series: Whimsical
  treats | Includes index. |
  Identifiers: LCCN 2020017586 | ISBN 9781510759510 (print) | ISBN
  9781510759527 (ebook)
Subjects: LCSH: Cookies. | Christmas cooking. | LCGFT: Cookbooks.
Classification: LCC TX772 .G25 2020 | DDC 641.86/54—dc23
LC record available at https://lccn.loc.gov/2020017586

Cover design by Daniel Brount
Cover photo by Cayla Gallagher

Print ISBN: 978-1-5107-5951-0
Ebook ISBN: 978-1-5107-5952-7

Printed in China

CONTENTS

OTHER TREATS & EXTRAS 145

DRINKS 189

Reindeer Marshmallows, page 141

*Snowflake Marshmallows,
page 137*

INTRODUCTION

Welcome to my third book in the series of Whimsical Treats! So far, we've baked tons of magical goodies in *Unicorn Food* and *Mermaid Food*, and now we're in the kitchen with Santa and his reindeer. Christmas is, by far, my favorite holiday and I've always wanted to write a Christmas cookbook. I kept coming up with more and more ideas; I felt like a kid in a candy shop!

You'll find here a selection of classic recipes and flavors, as well as some wintry treats like the Wintry Snowstorm Cake (page 5) and Cable Knit Cake (page 11). My Christmas Pudding Cake (page 33) is wonderfully festive, but I also love the glamor of silver and gold during the holidays, like in my Christmas Bauble Cakelettes (page 69).

You'll see I've used several shapes and sizes of piping tips when decorating with buttercream. These provide you with endless decorating possibilities and are so simple to use. If you're just starting to build your baking tool kit, I recommend purchasing a beginner's piping set, which usually includes several basic tips, a piping bag, and a coupler (a tool to attach the tips to the bag). All used here are quite common and should be easy to find.

I highly prefer using gel food coloring as it provides a deep, vibrant color with only a couple drops, whereas liquid food coloring requires you to use much more to achieve the same pigmentation. It can also change the consistency of your recipe and add a mild "food coloring" flavor—which you won't get with the gel. My one exception to this is the Red Velvet White Christmas Cake (page 37), which uses liquid red food coloring, because the cake likes the added moisture!

I genuinely hope you find joy and inspiration from this book, that you love the recipes, and, most important, I wish you the most wonderful holiday season! If you ever have any questions about any recipes found here or in my other books, don't hesitate to reach out to me on social media.

Lastly, thank you for picking up this book. Becoming a cookbook author has always been a dream of mine, and I never imagined that I would be fortunate enough to write multiple cookbooks so early on in my career. I am endlessly grateful for your support. Thank you for believing in me. I feel like the luckiest girl!

Gingerbread House Cake,
page 21

CAKES

WINTRY SNOWSTORM CAKE

This cake brings a blizzard right into your kitchen! It's a blueberry marble cake, topped with the most delicious cream cheese frosting. Hidden underneath the trees at the top are fresh strawberries, which cut through the sweetness of the cake and are juicy and refreshing! If you love the holidays, but aren't necessarily a fan of classic holiday flavors, this cake is for you.

Cake Batter:
1 cup unsalted butter, room temperature
2 cups sugar
3 teaspoons vanilla extract
6 large eggs
3 cups all-purpose flour
1 teaspoon baking soda
1 teaspoon salt
1½ cups sour cream
Blue food coloring
1 cup frozen blueberries

Cream Cheese Frosting:
16 ounces cream cheese, room temperature
1 cup unsalted butter, room temperature
2 teaspoons vanilla extract
7 cups confectioners' sugar

Blue and black food coloring
3 fresh strawberries
Silver star sprinkles

Bake the Cake:

1. Grease and flour 3 (6-inch) round cake pans and preheat the oven to 350°F.

2. Beat the butter and sugar with an electric mixer until pale and smooth. Add the vanilla extract and eggs one at a time, mixing with each addition.

3. In a separate bowl, combine the flour, baking soda, and salt. Add this to the batter in 2 additions, alternating with the sour cream.

4. Divide the batter in half. Dye one half blue (about 3 drops) and add the blueberries.

5. Spoon dollops of both colors of batter into your prepared pans. Gently swirl the dough with a knife to create a marble effect. Bake for 40 to 50 minutes, or until a skewer inserted into the centers comes out clean. Cool completely.

Make the Frosting:

1. Beat the cream cheese and butter in an electric mixer until pale and fluffy. Add the vanilla extract and beat until combined. Add the confectioners' sugar 1 cup at a time, then beat for 2 to 3 minutes, or until light and fluffy.

(Continued on next page)

Assembly:

1. Slice the tops and bottoms off the cakes to smooth the surface and remove any excess browning.

2. Stack the cakes, spreading about ½ cup of frosting between each layer. Then coat the entire cake in a thin layer of frosting. Place the cake in the fridge to chill for 20 minutes.

3. Take ⅓ of the remaining frosting and place it in a piping bag fitted with a #19 (small star) piping tip. Set aside.

4. Divide the remaining frosting into 3 bowls. Use just a couple drops of food coloring for the first bowl, then dye the other two progressively darker shades of blue. Use some black food coloring to help deepen the blue.

5. Pipe a small amount of white frosting around the base of the cake. Spread about 2 to 3 inches of light blue frosting directly above the white frosting, followed by 3 inches of medium blue frosting. Spread dark blue frosting the remaining way up the sides and on top of the cake.

6. Use a cake spatula to smooth the sides of the cake and gently blur the borders between each color. This will make it look like the night sky!

7. Next, pipe the white trees onto the cake. Start with the top of the tree, piping a dollop and dragging it upward, creating a triangle. Continue down the tree, creating a tall triangle. If you would like the tree to be fuller, add another layer of "branches" directly on top.

8. Trim the stem and tops off 3 strawberries, creating a flat base for them to rest on. Repeat the tree technique on the strawberries, starting at the top of the tree and working downward toward the base. Place a silver star sprinkle on top of each strawberry. Place the strawberries in the fridge until you are ready to serve the cake. Strawberries are quite juicy, so only add the strawberries to the cake right before serving. Juice may run into the frosting otherwise.

9. Place the remaining white frosting into a piping bag fitted with a #4 (round small) piping tip. Pipe round dots, or "snowflakes," all over the cake, spacing them farther apart as you move down the sides of the cake.

10. Top with the strawberries and enjoy!

Chocolate Snowflake Mousse Cake

MAKES A 9-INCH CAKE

This delicious cake uses dark chocolate, milk chocolate, and white chocolate! We use a cool stencil technique to create beautiful snowflakes on the surface, making this a showstopping dessert. If you love the holidays, but want to switch up the classic holiday flavors, this cake is for you!

Dark Chocolate Cake:
⅔ cup all-purpose flour
⅓ cup cocoa powder
⅔ cup sugar
¾ teaspoon baking soda
¾ teaspoon baking powder
¼ teaspoon salt
1 large egg
¼ cup milk
3 tablespoons oil
½ teaspoon vanilla extract
¼ cup water

Milk Chocolate Mousse:
2 teaspoons powdered gelatin
1½ tablespoons cold water
3 large egg whites
7 ounces whipping cream
2½ ounces milk
5 ounces good-quality milk chocolate

White Chocolate Mousse:
2 teaspoons powdered gelatin
1½ tablespoons water
3 large egg whites
7 ounces whipping cream
2½ ounces milk
5 ounces good-quality white chocolate
Snowflake paper cutouts
¼ cup cocoa powder, for dusting

Bake the Cake:

1. Preheat oven to 350°F. Place the flour, cocoa powder, sugar, baking soda, baking powder, and salt in the bowl of an electric mixer and mix on low speed until fully combined.

2. Add the egg, milk, oil, vanilla, and water and mix until smooth. Line the sides and bottom of a 9-inch springform pan with parchment paper and pour the batter into the pan.

3. Bake for 20 to 30 minutes, or until a skewer inserted into the center comes out clean. Place the pan on a cooling rack and cool completely in the pan.

4. Remove the cake from the pan and remove the parchment paper lining. Return the cake to the pan and set aside.

Make the Milk Chocolate Mousse:

1. Sprinkle the gelatin into the cold water and set aside.

2. Beat the egg whites until stiff peaks form. In a separate bowl, beat the whipping cream until soft peaks form and set both bowls aside.

3. Set a small saucepan to medium heat and add the milk. Just before the milk comes to a boil, turn off the heat and add the gelatin mixture. Once the gelatin has fully dissolved, add the milk chocolate and whisk until

(Continued on page 9)

fully melted. You may need to turn the heat back on to fully melt the chocolate. Add this mixture to the whipped cream and whisk to combine. Then add the egg whites and whisk to combine, making sure to keep the mixture as airy as possible. Pour the mousse on top of the chocolate cake and smooth the surface. Transfer the cake to the fridge to set for 2 hours.

Make the White Chocolate Mousse:

1. Follow the same steps for the Milk Chocolate Mousse, replacing the milk chocolate with white chocolate.

2. Once you have gently poured the white chocolate mousse onto the cake, transfer the cake to the fridge and set for 2½ hours.

To Decorate:

1. Place the paper snowflake cutouts onto the surface of the cake. To help with positioning, use some tape to create little handles on the corner of each snowflake.

2. Sift cocoa powder evenly over the entire surface of the cake. Gently remove the cutouts to reveal white snowflakes!

3. Gently unlatch the sides of the pan and slide it off the cake. Running a warm, damp dishcloth around the sides of the pan will make it easier to remove. To serve, slice the cake with a warm knife.

CABLE KNIT CAKE

This is one of my favorite cakes I've ever made! Knitted sweaters are the best part of winter, in my opinion, so a knitted cake is a must. This is a vanilla cranberry cake, topped with chocolate-covered marshmallows, which look just like pompoms!

Cake Batter:
1 cup unsalted butter, room temperature
2 cups sugar
3 teaspoons vanilla extract
6 large eggs
3 cups all-purpose flour
1 teaspoon baking soda
1 teaspoon salt
1½ cups sour cream
1 cup cranberries, fresh or frozen

Buttercream:
2 cups unsalted butter, room temperature
1 teaspoon vanilla extract, or seeds from
 1 vanilla bean
5 cups confectioners' sugar

Decorations:
4 jumbo marshmallows
1½ cups white candy melts, melted
1 cup white sprinkles

Bake the Cake:

1. Grease and flour 3 (6-inch) round cake pans, and preheat the oven to 350°F.

2. Beat the butter and sugar with an electric mixer until pale and smooth. Add the vanilla extract and eggs one at a time, mixing with each addition.

3. In a separate bowl, combine the flour, baking soda, and salt. Add this to the batter in 2 additions, alternating with the sour cream. Add the cranberries and fold to combine.

4. Spoon the batter into your prepared cake pans. Bake for 60 to 70 minutes, or until a skewer inserted into the centers comes out clean. Cool completely.

Make the Buttercream:

1. Beat the butter with an electric mixer until pale and fluffy. Add the vanilla extract and confectioners' sugar 1 cup at a time, beating with each addition.

Make the Decorations:

1. Insert a skewer into a jumbo marshmallow and fully submerge into the melted candy melts. The skewer should be 4 to 5 inches to secure into the cake—you can use a wooden skewer or a lollipop stick.

(Continued on next page)

2. Allow any excess candy melts to drip off, then roll in white sprinkles. It may take a few minutes for the candy melts to set, so keep the marshmallow in the bowl of sprinkles until the candy melt coating feels stiff.

3. Repeat with the remaining marshmallows and set aside. Try to resist eating them before you finish the cake!

Assembly:

1. Slice the tops and bottoms off the cakes to smooth the surface and remove any excess browning.

2. Spread some buttercream between each layer, stacking the cakes.

3. Coat the stacked cake in a thin layer of buttercream (this is your crumb coat—it will catch any excess cake crumbs). Chill the cake in the fridge for 20 minutes.

4. Place the remaining buttercream in piping bags fitted with #2A (medium-large round), #19 (small star), and #4 (small round) piping tips.

5. Use a long spatula or skewer to faintly make a straight vertical line down the cake. Pipe a pattern, following the visual guide, directly down the line. The line will ensure that your pattern stays straight. Repeat with the other patterns shown, making a faint line each time as a guide.

6. Once you have completely covered the cake, pipe little dollops using the #19 (small star) piping tip around the top edge of the cake.

7. Top the cake with the marshmallow pompoms, using the skewers to secure them to the cake. Enjoy!

Cinnamon Bun Cake

MAKES A 3-TIER CAKE, 14 CINNAMON BUNS TOTAL

The ultimate Christmas-morning treat! These homemade cinnamon buns are so warm and buttery and are topped with the best cream cheese glaze you will ever have. There is nothing like freshly baked cinnamon buns, and I'm certain that this cake will turn to crumbs in a matter of seconds.

Brioche Dough:

⅓ cup whole milk, warm

2¼ teaspoons active dry yeast

5 eggs, divided

3½ cups all-purpose flour, divided

⅓ cup sugar

1 teaspoon salt

3 sticks unsalted butter, room temperature, divided

Filling:

6 tablespoons granulated sugar

3½ teaspoons cinnamon

1 egg, beaten

1½ sticks unsalted butter

Icing:

8 ounces cream cheese, room temperature

1½ cups confectioners' sugar

4 tablespoons milk

1. Pour the milk, yeast, 1 egg, and 1 cup flour into the bowl of an electric mixer. Mix to combine, then sprinkle over another 1 cup flour. Let rise for 40 minutes.

2. Lightly beat the 4 remaining eggs, then add these to the dough along with the sugar, salt, and 1 cup flour. Place these into a mixer fitted with a dough hook and mix on low speed for 2 minutes. Add ½ cup flour and mix on medium speed for 15 minutes.

3. Reduce the speed to medium-low and gradually add 1½ sticks of butter. Increase the speed to medium-high and beat for 1 minute, then reduce the speed to medium and beat for 5 minutes.

4. Place the dough in a large, buttered bowl and cover with plastic wrap. Let rise for 2½ hours.

5. Deflate the dough, then replace the plastic wrap and place the bowl in the fridge. Let sit for 4 to 6 hours, or up to overnight.

6. Divide the dough in half. Place one ball of dough on a floured surface and roll the dough into an 11x13-inch rectangle. Evenly disperse half of the remaining butter onto the surface of the dough, then fold the dough into thirds, like a letter.

7. Roll the dough out into an 11x13-inch rectangle, then fold into thirds again. Wrap tightly in plastic wrap and place in the fridge for 30 minutes. Repeat with the remaining dough.

(Continued on next page)

8. Combine the sugar and cinnamon in a bowl and set aside.

9. Place one piece of dough on a floured surface and roll into an 11x13-inch rectangle. Brush the surface with the beaten egg. Sprinkle half of the cinnamon sugar onto the dough, leaving the top quarter of the dough bare. Roll the dough into a log, starting with the cinnamon sugar end and ending with the bare end. Wrap in plastic wrap and place in the freezer for 45 minutes. Repeat with the remaining dough. (Note: if you are making this for a party or a brunch, you can complete the previous steps a day in advance and start from step 10 on the day you are serving the cake.)

10. Divide the 1½ sticks butter between a 9-inch, 7-inch and 3½ inch–round baking tin (I used casserole dishes and they worked great, so no need to stress if you don't have baking tins in these sizes).

11. Unwrap the logs and slice them into 1½ inch–thick buns, making 14 buns. Place 7 buns in the 9-inch tin, 6 buns in the 7-inch tin, and 1 bun in the 3½-inch tin. Let the buns rise at room temperature for 1½ hours.

12. Bake the buns at 350°F for 35 to 40 minutes, until golden brown, removing the bun in the smallest tin after 20 minutes. Place a baking sheet lined with parchment paper on the rack under the cinnamon buns to catch any drips.

13. As soon as the cinnamon buns are finished baking, flip them out onto a wire rack. Excess butter may drip out, so make sure to place some paper towels under the rack. Turn the buns right side up, and let slightly cool.

14. To make the icing, place the cream cheese in a bowl and beat with an electric mixer for 2 minutes, until the cream cheese is fluffy. Add the confectioners' sugar and milk and beat until combined.

Giant Christmas Tree Cake

MAKES AN 8-INCH BASE AND ABOUT 15 INCHES HIGH

As impressive looking as this cake is, it is also delicious! This is my favorite vanilla cake recipe because it is so moist and tender, yet sturdy enough to stack.

Cake Batter:
2 cups unsalted butter, room temperature
4 cups sugar
2 tablespoons vanilla extract
12 large eggs
6 cups all-purpose flour
2 teaspoons baking soda
2 teaspoons salt
3 cups sour cream

Buttercream:
6 cups unsalted butter, room temperature
3 teaspoons vanilla extract
15 cups confectioners' sugar
Green food coloring
Jujube gummies

Bake the Cake:
1. Grease and flour 4 (6-inch) round cake pans, and 2 (8-inch) round cake pans. Preheat the oven to 350°F.

2. Beat the butter and sugar with an electric mixer until pale and smooth. Add the vanilla extract and eggs one at a time, mixing with each addition.

3. In a separate bowl, combine the flour, baking soda, and salt. Add this to the batter in 2 additions, alternating with the sour cream.

4. Spoon the batter into your prepared pans. Bake for 30 minutes, or until a skewer inserted into the centers comes out clean. Cool completely.

Make the Buttercream:
1. Beat the butter with an electric mixer until pale and fluffy. Add the vanilla extract and confectioners' sugar 1 cup at a time, beating with each addition.

2. Dye the buttercream green (about 3 drops) and place it into a piping bag fitted with a large, star-shaped piping tip (#4B).

Assembly:
1. Slice the tops and bottoms off the cakes to smooth the surface and remove any excess browning.

2. Stack the 8-inch cakes, spreading some buttercream between each layer. Stick some bubble tea straws into the center of the cakes and snip with scissors until they

(Continued on page 19)

are as tall as the cakes (these are wider than skewers, and hollow, so will keep the cake sturdier—you can use skewers if needed). Place a 6-inch cake board on top and cover with buttercream.

3. Stack 3 of the 6-inch cakes on top, spreading buttercream between each layer. Stick 3 more bubble tea straws inside and press all the way down, until they hit the cake board. Place the final layer of cake on top.

4. Carve the cake into a cone shape. Don't worry about the top not being too pointy, we will address this next!

5. Place the cake scraps in a bowl and beat with an electric mixer until the cake has crumbled. Add some buttercream and mix until the cake sticks together and can easily be molded. Stick another bubble tea straw into the center of the cake, making it as tall as you'd like the cake to be. Mold the cake mixture around the straw to create the top of the tree.

6. Starting at the base of the cake, pipe buttercream dollops in rows. Once you've covered the entire cake, decorate it with jujube gummies, to look like Christmas tree lights. Enjoy!

GINGERBREAD HOUSE CAKE

SERVES 6-8

Gingerbread houses are the quintessential holiday treat, so I wanted to create a cute twist here! This is a chocolate gingerbread cake iced with chocolate gingerbread buttercream. This is also easier to decorate because you don't have to fuss with royal icing!

Cake Batter:

2 cups all-purpose flour

2 cups sugar

¾ cup cocoa powder

2 teaspoons baking powder

1½ teaspoons baking soda

1–2 tablespoons Gingerbread Spice Mix (page 147)

1 teaspoon salt

1 cup milk

½ cup vegetable oil

2 large eggs

2 teaspoons vanilla extract

1 cup boiling water

Buttercream (page 11)

1 tablespoon Gingerbread Spice Mix (page 147)

¼ cup cocoa powder

Brown food coloring

Candies, sprinkles, icing decorations, and Mini Wheats

Bake the Cake:

1. Grease 4 (6-inch) round baking pans. Preheat the oven to 350°F.

2. Place the flour, sugar, cocoa powder, baking powder, baking soda, Gingerbread Spice Mix, and salt in a large bowl and mix together.

3. Add the milk, vegetable oil, eggs, and vanilla extract and mix with an electric mixer until combined.

4. Slowly add the boiling water and mix until well combined.

5. Divide the batter evenly between the pans and bake for 30 to 35 minutes, until a skewer inserted into the center comes out clean. Cool for 15 minutes in the pan, then turn onto a wire rack and cool completely.

Assembly:

1. Place about 1 cup of buttercream into a piping bag fitted with a small, star-shaped piping tip.

2. Add the Gingerbread Spice Mix, cocoa powder, and a couple drops brown food coloring to the remaining buttercream. Mix well.

3. Slice the tops off 3 of the cakes. Cut the edges to shape them into squares. Don't throw out the extra cake—you can use this for cake pops!

4. Cut the final cake into a roof shape, using the other cakes as a guide to shape it into a square.

5. Stack the cakes, spreading some brown buttercream between each layer. Cover the cake in a thin layer of buttercream, then place the cake in the fridge for 20 to 30 minutes, until the buttercream has stiffened.

6. Cover the entire cake in a thick, generous layer of brown buttercream. Decorate the house with the white icing, which will look like royal icing on traditional gingerbread houses. Add some Mini Wheats for roof tiles and some gummies or sugar decorations for the rest of the house. Enjoy!

WREATH BUNDT CAKE

MAKES 1 BUNDT CAKE

This is such a simple recipe, but it has amazing visual impact! This doesn't require any fussing with cake layers, so it's a great dessert to make with your little one or if you're short on time.

1 cup unsalted butter, room temperature

2 cups sugar

3 teaspoons vanilla extract

6 large eggs

3 cups all-purpose flour

3 tablespoons matcha green tea powder

1 teaspoon baking soda

1 teaspoon salt

1½ cups sour cream

3 tablespoons matcha green tea powder

Buttercream (page 11)

1 red Fruit by the Foot

Festive candies and sprinkles

Bake the Cake:

1. Grease and flour a Bundt cake pan and preheat the oven to 350°F.

2. Beat the butter and sugar with an electric mixer until pale and smooth. Add the vanilla extract and add the eggs one at a time, mixing with each addition.

3. In a separate bowl, combine the flour, matcha green tea powder, baking soda, and salt. Add this to the batter in 2 additions, alternating with the sour cream.

4. Spoon the batter into your prepared pan. Bake for 45 to 60 minutes, or until a skewer inserted into the cake comes out clean. Invert the pan onto a wire rack, remove the pan, and cool the cake completely.

Assembly:

1. Add the matcha green tea powder to your buttercream and mix well.

2. Place about ¾ of buttercream into a piping bag fitted with a large, open star-shaped piping tip.

3. Place the cake on your work surface and, if desired, round the edges of the cake with a serrated knife, creating a wreath-like appearance.

4. Cover the entire surface of the cake in a thin layer of buttercream. This will help the piped buttercream stick better.

5. Using the buttercream in the piping bag, pipe tufts of buttercream all over the cake.

6. Create a bow out of the Fruit by the Foot and stick to the cake. Decorate with festive candy and sprinkles and enjoy!

REINDEER CAKE

A festive spin on my classic Unicorn Cake (check out my first book for that one!)—this sweet little reindeer tastes like vanilla and cherries and is completely free of fondant! For the antlers and ears, we're using homemade gingerbread cookies, sprinkled with turbinado sugar to give them a delicious crunch. Rudolph is knocking on your kitchen window and wants to join your dessert table this year!

Cake Batter:
1 cup unsalted butter, room temperature
2 cups sugar
Zest from 1 lemon
3 teaspoons vanilla extract
6 large eggs
3 cups all-purpose flour
1 teaspoon baking soda
1 teaspoon salt
1½ cups sour cream

Gingerbread Cookie Dough (page 183)
2 lollipop sticks
¼ cup turbinado sugar
Buttercream (page 11)
½ cup cherry jam
Brown, black, red, and green food coloring
1 red melting wafer

Bake the Cake:

1. Grease and flour 3 (6-inch) round cake pans and preheat the oven to 350°F.

2. Beat the butter and sugar with an electric mixer until pale and smooth. Add the lemon zest, vanilla extract, and eggs one at a time, mixing with each addition.

3. In a separate bowl, combine the flour, baking soda, and salt. Add this to the batter in 2 additions, alternating with the sour cream.

4. Spoon the batter into your prepared pans. Bake for 40 to 50 minutes, or until a skewer inserted into the centers comes out clean. Cool completely.

Make the Decorations:

1. Roll the Gingerbread Cookie Dough out on a floured surface. Refer to my photo on the next page and use a sharp knife to draw 2 antlers and 2 ears. The ears should point downward at the base, so that they can easily be stuck into the cake.

2. Place a lollipop stick into the last 3 to 4 inches of the antlers and gently press to secure them to the cookie dough.

3. Generously sprinkle some turbinado sugar onto the antlers and press them into the dough with your hands.

(Continued on next page)

4. Bake the cookies at 350°F for 10 minutes, or until the edges are lightly browned. Cool completely.

Assembly:

1. Slice the tops and bottoms off the cakes to smooth the surface and remove any excess browning.

2. Stack the cakes, spreading some buttercream between each layer. Add a couple dollops of cherry jam on top of the buttercream before placing the next cake layer on top.

3. Coat the cake in a thin layer of buttercream to catch any excess cake crumbs. Chill the cake in the fridge for 20 minutes.

4. Dye half of the remaining buttercream brown (about 6 drops). Cover the entire cake in a generous layer of brown buttercream and smooth the surface.

5. Place half of the remaining white buttercream into a piping bag fitted with a #2A (large, round) piping tip. Pipe and fill in the areas for the eyes and smooth with a knife. Then pipe 6 dots on the forehead.

6. Dye 2 tablespoons of remaining buttercream black and place in a piping bag fitted with a #9 (medium, round) piping tip. Pipe the reindeer's eyes onto the white area.

7. Place the red melting wafer between the eyes as the nose.

8. Divide the remaining white buttercream in half, and dye one half red and the rest green. Place the red buttercream in a piping bag fitted with a #9 (medium, round) piping tip and place the green buttercream in a piping bag fitted with a #6B (large, open star) piping tip.

9. Stick the antlers and ears into the cake. You may need to use a knife to create an opening to insert the ears. Pipe the green and red buttercream around the ears and antlers, as holly and berries.

Surprise-Inside Pine Tree Cake

MAKES A 9-INCH POUND CAKE

This cake is so much fun! It looks like a vanilla pound cake, but slice into it and a beautiful pine tree says hello! This may seem like a tricky technique, but it's actually incredibly easy to do.

Green Cake:
1 cup all-purpose flour
1¾ teaspoons baking powder
¼ teaspoon salt
¼ cup unsalted butter, room temperature
½ cup granulated sugar
1 teaspoon vanilla extract
1 large egg
½ cup milk
Green food coloring

White Cake:
2 cups all-purpose flour
3½ teaspoons baking powder
½ teaspoon salt
½ cup unsalted butter, room temperature
1 cup granulated sugar
1 teaspoon vanilla extract
2 large eggs
1 cup milk

Frosting:
½ cup unsalted butter, room temperature
½ teaspoon vanilla extract
1¼ cups confectioners' sugar
Silver and green sprinkles

Make the Green Trees:

1. Grease a 9x9-inch square baking pan and preheat the oven to 350°F.

2. Combine the flour, baking powder, and salt in a bowl.

3. In a separate bowl, cream the butter with an electric mixer until pale and fluffy. Add the sugar and mix until combined. Add the vanilla extract and egg and mix well.

4. Add the flour mixture in 2 additions, alternating with the milk. Add the green food coloring to dye the batter your desired shade of green.

5. Pour the batter into your prepared pan and bake for 20 minutes, or until fully cooked. Cool the cake in the pan for 10 minutes, then remove from the pan and transfer to a wire rack. Cool completely.

6. Use a pine tree–shaped cookie cutter or a paper stencil to cut out 6 to 7 trees from the green cake. Set aside.

Make the White Batter:

1. Combine the flour, baking powder, and salt in a bowl.

2. In a separate bowl, cream the butter with an electric mixer until pale and fluffy. Add the sugar and mix until combined. Add the vanilla extract and egg and mix well. Add the flour mixture in 2 additions, alternating with the milk.

(Continued on page 29)

Bake the Cake:

1. Grease a 9-inch loaf pan and pour ⅓ of the white batter into the bottom of the pan. Line up the green trees in the center of the loaf pan, making sure they are pressed together to create a long, solid shape.

2. Spoon the remaining white batter around the sides and top of the trees, making sure they are fully covered.

3. Bake for 50 to 60 minutes, or until a skewer inserted into all edges of the cake comes out clean. This style of cake takes longer to cook than usual, so make sure to check all sides of the white cake to make sure they are cooked. If it is still raw, pop the cake back in the oven for 5 minutes at a time. Allow the cake to cool in the pan for 20 minutes, then remove from the pan and transfer to a wire rack. Cool completely.

Make the Frosting:

1. Place the butter in a bowl and beat with an electric mixer until pale and fluffy. Add the vanilla extract and beat until combined. Add the confectioners' sugar and beat until pale and fluffy, 3 to 4 minutes.

To Decorate:

1. Spread the frosting onto the cake and top with silver and green sprinkles.

2. Slice to reveal pine trees inside!

Ugly Christmas Sweater Cake

MAKES A 9X13 CAKE

This cake is full of Christmas fun! Bring this to an ugly Christmas sweater party and you'll be the guest of honor. Alternatively, host your own Ugly Christmas Sweater Cake party. Prepare several knitted cake canvases and invite your guests to decorate their own.

Cake Batter:

1 cup unsalted butter, room temperature

2 cups brown sugar

3 teaspoons vanilla extract

6 large eggs

3 cups all-purpose flour

1 teaspoon baking soda

1 teaspoon salt

2 tablespoons cinnamon

1½ cups sour cream

Buttercream:

4 cups unsalted butter, room temperature

2 teaspoons vanilla extract, or seeds from 2 vanilla beans

1 tablespoon cinnamon

7½ cups confectioners' sugar

Green and red food coloring

3 green candy melts

¼ cup round candies (M&M's would work)

Large star sprinkles

Bake the Cake:

1. Grease and flour a 9x13-inch cake pan and preheat the oven to 350°F.

2. Beat the butter and brown sugar with an electric mixer until pale and smooth. Add the vanilla extract and eggs one at a time, mixing with each addition.

3. In a separate bowl, combine the flour, baking soda, salt, and cinnamon. Add this to the batter in 2 additions, alternating with the sour cream.

4. Spoon the batter into your prepared cake pan. Bake for 40 to 50 minutes, or until a skewer inserted into the center comes out clean. Cool completely.

Make the Buttercream:

1. Beat the butter with an electric mixer until pale and fluffy. Add the vanilla extract, cinnamon, and confectioners' sugar 1 cup at a time, beating with each addition.

2. Reserve 1 cup white buttercream. Place it in a piping bag fitted with a #6B (large, open star) piping tip. Dye ½ cup buttercream green (about 3 drops). Place it in a piping bag fitted with a #8 (small/medium round) piping tip. Dye the remaining buttercream red (about 4 drop).

(Continued on next page)

Assembly:

1. Slice the top off the cake to smooth the surface. Slice the cake in half to create two 6½x9-inch cakes. Stack the cakes, spreading about ⅔ cup red buttercream between the layers.

2. Coat the cake in an even layer of red buttercream. Place the remaining buttercream in a piping bag fitted with a #10 (medium, round) piping tip.

3. Mark a wide V-shape at the top of the cake, for the neck of the sweater.

4. Using the same technique as in the Cable Knit Cake (page 11), pipe a cable pattern all over the cake. Unlike the Cable Knit Cake, all the cables on this cake will be the same size and style.

5. Once the cake is covered in cables, pipe dollops with the white buttercream around the collar of the sweater and all the way down the front.

6. Place the green candy melts onto the white buttercream. Place the remaining white buttercream into a piping bag fitted with a #4 (small, round) piping tip. Pipe an "x" in the center of each candy melt to make them look like buttons!

7. Use the green buttercream to pipe swirls onto each side of the sweater. Stick the colorful candies onto the green, to look like Christmas lights. Stick some star sprinkles into any bare spaces you see.

8. Enjoy your delicious, ugly sweater!

CHRISTMAS PUDDING CAKE

SERVES 6-8

Christmas pudding is such a classic treat, but it can take ages to make! This cake is a cute, chocolaty alternative. We are using my classic chocolate cake recipe, which is moist and flavorful. Make sure to bookmark this page, because this chocolate cake will be calling your name for many days to come!

Cake Batter:
¾ cup cocoa powder + extra for coating
2 cups all-purpose flour
2 cups sugar
2 teaspoons baking powder
1½ teaspoons baking soda
1 teaspoon salt
2 teaspoons Gingerbread Spice Mix (page 147)
1 cup milk
½ cup vegetable oil
2 large eggs
2 teaspoons vanilla extract
1 cup boiling water

1 cup frozen cranberries, thawed
⅓ cup candied ginger, finely chopped
⅓ cup marzipan
Red and green food coloring

Chocolate Buttercream:
2 cups unsalted butter, room temperature
2 tablespoons vanilla extract
½ cup milk
4 cups confectioners' sugar
1½ cups cocoa powder

Vanilla Buttercream:
½ cup unsalted butter, room temperature
½ teaspoon vanilla extract
1 cup confectioners' sugar

Bake the Cake:
1. Grease and flour 3 (6-inch) round baking pans, but use cocoa powder instead of flour to coat the pans. This will keep the outsides of the cakes looking rich and chocolaty, instead of pale and floury. Preheat the oven to 350°F.

2. Place the flour, sugar, cocoa powder, baking powder, baking soda, salt, and Gingerbread Spice Mix in a large bowl and mix together.

3. Add the milk, vegetable oil, eggs, and vanilla extract and mix with an electric mixer until combined.

4. Slowly add the boiling water and mix until well combined.

5. Divide the batter evenly between the pans and bake for 30 to 35 minutes, until a skewer inserted into the centers comes out clean. Cool for 15 minutes in the pans, then turn onto a wire rack and cool completely.

Make the Chocolate Buttercream:
1. Beat the butter with an electric mixer until pale and fluffy. Add the vanilla extract and milk and mix well. Add the confectioners' sugar and cocoa powder 1 cup at a time, beating with each addition.

(Continued on page 35)

Make the Vanilla Buttercream:

1. Beat the butter with an electric mixer until pale and fluffy. Add the vanilla extract and mix well. Add the confectioners' sugar 1 cup at a time, beating with each addition.

Assembly:

1. Slice the tops off the cakes to smooth the surface. Stack the cakes and use a serrated knife to carve them into a sphere.

2. Spread some chocolate buttercream between each layer. Scatter some cranberries and ginger onto the buttercream before placing the next layer of cake on top.

3. Coat the cake in a thin layer of buttercream. This will catch any excess cake crumbs. Chill the cake in the fridge for 20 minutes.

4. Coat the chilled cake in a thick, generous layer of buttercream and smooth the surface.

5. Spread some white buttercream on top to look like the glaze on a Christmas pudding.

6. Dye ⅔ of the marzipan red (about 3 to 4 drops) and ⅓ green (about 2 to 3 drops). Shape the red marzipan into 3 holly berries. Shape the green marzipan into 2 holly leaves. Place on top of the cake.

RED VELVET WHITE CHRISTMAS CAKE

SERVES 6-8

Red velvet cakes are loved all over the globe, and this recipe is the best of the best! The cake is so delicate and the cream cheese frosting is seriously addictive. Add some delicate royal icing snowflakes and this cake is perfect for the holidays!

Snowflakes:
½ pound confectioners' sugar
2½ tablespoons meringue powder
¼ cup water
Red food coloring

Cake Batter:
3¾ cups cake flour
¼ cup + 2 tablespoons cocoa powder
1½ teaspoons salt
2¼ cups sugar
2¼ cups canola oil
1½ teaspoons vanilla extract
¼ cup + 2 tablespoons red food coloring
3 large eggs
1½ cups buttermilk
¾ teaspoons baking soda
3 teaspoons white vinegar

Cream Cheese Frosting:
18 ounces cream cheese, room temperature
3¼ cups unsalted butter, room temperature
2 teaspoons vanilla extract
5 cups confectioners' sugar

Make the Snowflakes:

1. Combine the confectioners' sugar, meringue powder, and water in a bowl and beat with an electric mixer for 7 minutes, until the mixture stays on the surface for several seconds when drizzled.

2. Dye the frosting red and place in a piping bag fitted with a #2 (small round) piping tip.

3. Pipe snowflakes onto a baking sheet lined with parchment paper. Allow the icing to dry overnight, until very stiff.

Bake the Cake:

1. Grease and flour 2 (9-inch) round cake pans, and 1 (9-inch) square cake pan. Preheat the oven to 350°F.

2. Whisk together the cake flour, cocoa powder, and salt.

3. In a separate bowl, beat the sugar and oil with an electric mixer. Add the vanilla, food coloring, and eggs one at a time, beating well with each addition. Add the flour mixture in 2 additions, alternating with the buttermilk.

4. Combine the baking soda and vinegar in a small bowl, then add to the batter and mix well.

5. Pour into your prepared pans. Bake for 30 to 35 minutes, or until a skewer inserted into the centers comes out clean. Cool completely.

(Continued on next page)

Make the Frosting:

1. Beat the cream cheese and butter with an electric mixer until pale and fluffy. Add the vanilla extract and confectioners' sugar 1 cup at a time until fluffy.

Assembly:

1. Use a serrated knife to trim the 9-inch square cake into two 4½-inch circles. Trim the tops and sides off the 2 small and 2 large round cakes to flatten the surfaces and remove any excess browning. Spread some frosting between the two large cakes to layer, then cover in a generous layer of frosting. Place in the fridge to chill. Repeat with the small cakes.

2. Stack the small cake on top of the large cake and, if necessary, spread some extra frosting on top of the cake to conceal the seam between the two cakes.

3. Very gently peel the snowflakes off the parchment paper and stick them to the cake. If necessary, use some extra frosting to prop up the snowflakes. Enjoy!

GINGERBREAD VILLAGE CAKE

MAKES 1 CAKE

The base of this cake is so warm and tastes just like Christmas. Combine it with the jam-filled houses and mascarpone frosting, and you've got a spectacular cake, which requires minimal decorating. The light dusting of confectioners' sugar beautifully highlights the details on the little houses and looks like a fresh dusting of snow. This was the cake I made for my first television appearance!

Cake Batter:
1 cup boiling water
2 teaspoons baking soda
2½ cups flour
2 teaspoons ginger
1½ teaspoons cinnamon
½ teaspoon cloves
½ teaspoon nutmeg
½ teaspoon salt
½ cup unsalted butter, room temperature
⅔ cup brown sugar
1 cup molasses
⅓ cup candied ginger, finely chopped
2 eggs

Frosting:
¾ cup unsalted butter, room temperature
½ pound cream cheese, room temperature
1 cup confectioners' sugar
½ teaspoon vanilla extract
½ teaspoon orange zest
Pinch of cinnamon
4 ounces mascarpone cheese, room temperature
¼ cup candied ginger, finely chopped
⅓ cup ginger (or pear) jam
Fresh rosemary, for garnish
Confectioners' sugar, for dusting

Bake the Cake:
1. Preheat the oven to 350°F.

2. Mix together the boiling water and baking soda. Separately, sift together the flour, spices, and salt.

3. Beat the butter with an electric mixer until pale and fluffy. Add the brown sugar and keep beating until fluffy. Add the molasses, baking soda mixture, flour mixture, and candied ginger. Add the eggs and beat until combined.

4. Butter and flour a 9-inch round cake pan and a mini house cakelette pan (check Amazon or Nordic Ware). Fill each tiny house mold ¾ of the way full, then pour the remaining batter into the round cake pan. Bake for 30 to 35 minutes until a skewer inserted into the cakes comes out clean. Transfer the cakes to a wire rack and cool completely.

Make the Frosting:
1. Beat the butter and cream cheese in an electric mixer until pale and fluffy. Add the confectioners' sugar, vanilla extract, orange zest, and cinnamon and mix until combined. Add the mascarpone cheese and mix until just combined.

(Continued on page 41)

Assembly:

1. Slice the round cake into 2 layers. Use a small spoon to scoop about 1 tablespoon of cake out of the bottom of each house. This will create a little compartment to fill with jam in step 3.

2. Spread frosting between the 2 layers, adding enough frosting to make the filling look like fluffy snow. Sprinkle the candied ginger on top of the frosting filling. Spread a very thin layer of frosting on the top layer, leaving the sides bare. Dust the surface in an even layer of confectioners' sugar.

3. Fill the holes in the houses with ginger jam and arrange them on the surface of the cake. Stick rosemary around the houses to look like pine trees and remove some frosting in front of the houses to look like footpaths.

4. Dust the entire cake in a thin layer of confectioners' sugar to look like fresh snow.

No-Bake Gingerbread Man Cheesecake

MAKES A 9-INCH CHEESECAKE

Cheesecake isn't usually a traditional holiday dessert, but this recipe will change your mind! This no-bake cheesecake has a buttery gingerbread base with a smooth and creamy gingerbread filling. For an extra touch, it is topped with homemade chocolate gingerbread men.

Cheesecake Base:
5 tablespoons unsalted butter, melted

2⅓ cups finely crumbled gingerbread men

Cheesecake Filling:
1¾ cups cream cheese, room temperature

6½ tablespoons sugar

1¾ cups whipping cream

¼ cup lemon juice

½ teaspoon vanilla extract

5 teaspoons Gingerbread Spice Mix (page 147)

2 teaspoons powdered gelatin

2½ tablespoons water

Topping:
4 ounces semisweet chocolate, melted

1 teaspoon Gingerbread Spice Mix (page 147)

Cocoa powder, for dusting

Make the Cheesecake Base:
1. Mix together the melted butter and crumbled gingerbread men, then press them into the bottom of a 9-inch springform pan. Place this in the fridge while you make the filling.

Make the Filling:
1. Place the cream cheese in a bowl and beat with an electric mixer until smooth. Add the sugar and combine. Then add the whipping cream, lemon juice, vanilla extract, and Gingerbread Spice Mix and mix until smooth. Combine the gelatin and water in a small bowl and microwave for 30 seconds. Add to the filling, and mix together until fully combined.

2. Pour the filling into the cake pan and return to the fridge to chill until set (approx. 3 hours).

To Serve:
1. Combine the semisweet chocolate and Gingerbread Spice Mix and pour into 8 gingerbread man–shaped molds. Place in the fridge until set, about 1 to 2 hours.

2. Run a warm, damp dishcloth around the outside of the cheesecake pan, then run a sharp knife inside the pan, between the edge of the cake and the walls of the pan. Gently remove the sides of the pan from the cake.

3. Gently place 4 chocolate gingerbread men on top of the cake. Dust the entire surface with cocoa powder. Remove the gingerbread men to reveal their shapes, then add 4 clean gingerbread men, shifting their positions to create a pattern of alternating chocolate gingerbread men and their outlines.

4. Slice and enjoy!

Santa Sack Red Velvet Crepe Cake

MAKES 1 CREPE CAKE

These are Japanese-style crepes and they are delicately sweet. Layer them with cream cheese frosting and top with a variety of fruit and candy for an unforgettable dessert! We're adding the Peppermint Present truffles (page 117) as an extra special touch!

Crepe Batter:
1¾ cups all-purpose flour
½ cup potato starch
¼ cup sugar
½ tablespoon cocoa powder
2½ cups milk
A few drops vanilla extract
Red food coloring

Cream Filling:
9 ounces cream cheese, room temperature
¼ cup unsalted butter, room temperature
1 cup confectioners' sugar
Ribbon
Fresh fruit
Peppermint Present Truffles (page 117)

Make the Crepes:

1. Place the flour, potato starch, sugar, and cocoa powder in a bowl and lightly beat with an electric mixture. This will break up lumps and does the same thing as sifting the ingredients. Gradually add the milk, mixing with each addition. Then add the vanilla extract and a few drops of red food coloring, mixing well until the batter is smooth.

2. Set a lightly greased frying pan to medium heat and pour in enough batter to cover the bottom of the pan. Bring the heat down to low and place a lid on the pan. Cook the crepe until the surface is fully cooked, about 1 to 2 minutes.

3. Gently loosen the edges of the crepe from the pan using a chopstick or spatula, then flip the crepe out onto a plate. Continue with the remaining batter—you should be able to make about 15 crepes. Allow the crepes to fully cool. Using a plate as a guide, cut the crepes into clean circles.

Make the Cream Cheese Filling:

1. Beat the cream cheese and butter until smooth. Gradually add the confectioners' sugar until fully combined, then beat until smooth and fluffy.

Assembly:

1. Place one crepe face down on a flat surface. Arrange 5 crepes around the perimeter, slightly

(Continued on next page)

overlapping the middle crepe. Spread some cream cheese filling in between the layers to seal the crepes together. Place another crepe over the middle one and spread some filling evenly on top. Place another crepe on top and spread some more cream cheese over the surface. Repeat until all of the crepes are used up.

2. Fold the 5 overlapped crepes up the side and on top of the cake and secure them with a ribbon wrapped around the cake. Fold the edges back to look like a sack. Place the remaining cream cheese filling in a piping bag and pipe some more filling into the sack.

3. Decorate with fresh fruit and Peppermint Present Truffles and enjoy!

SNOWFLAKE SWISS ROLL CAKE

MAKES A 15-INCH CAKE

This Swiss roll cake is a beautiful vibrant blue and is perfect for the holiday season. To tell you the truth, I was intimidated by roll cakes for so long because I was nervous I'd break them, but this recipe couldn't be any easier! Just follow the steps and you'll have a flawless Swiss roll cake every single time.

Pattern:
3 tablespoons unsalted butter, room
   temperature
½ cup confectioners' sugar
3 large egg whites
¼ teaspoon vanilla extract
⅔ cup all-purpose flour

Cake Batter:
6 large eggs, yolks and whites separated
Pinch of salt
1 cup granulated sugar
2 teaspoons vanilla extract
5 tablespoons unsalted butter, melted and
   cooled
1 cup all-purpose flour
Blue food coloring

Filling:
1 cup whipping cream, cold
2 tablespoons confectioners' sugar
1 teaspoon vanilla extract

Make the Pattern:

1. Beat the butter with an electric mixer until light and fluffy. Add the confectioners' sugar and beat until combined. Add the egg whites and vanilla extract and beat until combined. Add the flour on low speed.

2. Place the batter into a piping bag fitted with a #8 (small round) piping tip.

3. Line a Swiss roll or jelly roll pan with parchment paper. Pipe snowflakes all over the paper—use my photo as an example.

4. Transfer the pan to the freezer for 30 minutes.

Make the Cake Batter:

1. Preheat the oven to 350°F.

2. Beat the 6 egg whites and salt with an electric mixer until soft peaks form. Add half of the granulated sugar and beat until stiff, glossy peaks are formed.

3. In a separate bowl, beat the egg yolks and remaining sugar with an electric mixer until pale and doubled in volume. Gradually add the vanilla extract and butter and mix until well combined.

4. Add the flour to the batter in 2 additions, alternating with the egg whites. Using just a couple drops of food coloring, dye the batter pale blue and gently fold to combine.

(Continued on page 49)

5. Pour the batter into the Swiss roll cake pan, on top of the pattern. Gently smooth the surface and bake for 13 to 15 minutes, until the edges are golden.

6. Dust a large sheet of wax paper with confectioners' sugar. As soon as the cake comes out of the oven, invert it onto the wax paper. Peel off the top layer of parchment paper, place another layer of wax paper on top, then invert again, so that the patterned side is facing down. Remove the wax paper, and, starting at one long end, gently roll the cake up. Wrap in a kitchen towel and cool completely.

Make the Filling:
1. Beat the whipping cream with an electric mixer until soft peaks form. Add the confectioners' sugar and vanilla extract and beat until stiff peaks form.

Assembly:
1. Once cooled, gently unroll the cake and peel off the wax paper. Spread the filling onto the surface and roll the cake back up again.

2. Wrap the cake in plastic wrap and chill in the fridge for 4 hours, or up to overnight.

3. Slice off the ends to create a clean look and enjoy!

Candy Cane Unicorn Cake

Unicorn cakes are loved by so many that I knew I needed to make a Christmas version! This unicorn is made with red, white, and green cake and topped with a matching horn. Unicorn cakes traditionally use quite a bit of fondant, but this cake is fondant-free! Every element is delicious, festive, and ready for holiday snacking.

Cake Batter:
1 cup unsalted butter, room temperature
2 cups sugar
3 teaspoons vanilla extract
6 large eggs
3 cups all-purpose flour
1 teaspoon baking soda
1 teaspoon salt
1½ cups sour cream
Red and green food coloring

Buttercream:
3 cups unsalted butter, room temperature
1½ teaspoons vanilla extract
2 teaspoons peppermint extract
7 cups confectioners' sugar
Black and red food coloring
½ cup marzipan

Red and green food coloring
Lollipop stick
1 jumbo marshmallow
Silver sanding sugar
Candy canes
Snowflake candies
Silver and white sprinkles

Bake the Cake:

1. Grease and flour 3 (6-inch) round cake pans, and preheat the oven to 350°F.

2. Beat the butter and sugar with an electric mixer until pale and smooth. Add the vanilla extract and eggs one at a time, mixing with each addition.

3. In a separate bowl, combine the flour, baking soda, and salt. Add to the batter in 2 additions, alternating with the sour cream. Divide the batter into 3 bowls. Using about 4 drops of each, dye one bowl red, one bowl green, and leave the remaining bowl white.

4. Spoon the batter into your prepared cake pans. Bake for 20 to 30 minutes, or until a skewer inserted into the centers comes out clean. Cool completely.

Make the Buttercream:

1. Beat the butter with an electric mixer until pale and fluffy. Add the extracts and mix until combined. Add the confectioners' sugar 1 cup at a time, mixing with each addition. Then beat for 3 to 5 minutes, until fluffy.

Make the Horn:

1. Divide the marzipan into 3 balls. Using 1 to 2 drops of each color, dye one ball red, one ball green, and leave the remaining ball white. Roll each ball into a thin, 5-inch-long log.

2. Twist the three together to create a horn shape. Then insert a lollipop stick into the bottom of the horn, making sure about 3 to 4 inches of the stick is still visible. This will be used to secure it to the cake. Place the horn on a plate lined with plastic wrap and set aside to stiffen while you decorate the cake.

(Continued on next page)

Assembly:

1. Slice the tops and bottoms off the cakes to remove any excess browning. Then slice each cake in half, to create a total of 6 layers. Stack them in your desired order, spreading about ⅓ cup buttercream between each layer. Coat the entire cake in a thin layer of buttercream, then place in the fridge to chill for 20 minutes.

2. Once chilled, cover the entire cake in a thick layer of buttercream and smooth the surface.

3. Dye ¼ cup of buttercream black. Place it in a piping bag fitted with a #4 (small, round) piping tip. Divide the remaining buttercream into 2 bowls. Dye one bowl red. Place both the red and white buttercream into a piping bag fitted with a #2D (large flower/star) piping tip. Add both colors in a vertical position, so that each color creates a vertical stripe inside the bag.

4. Using the red and white buttercream, pipe the mane onto the unicorn, starting at its forehead and working all the way down the back of the cake. Alternate between piping swirls and dollops to create a fabulous mane!

5. Slice the jumbo marshmallow in half diagonally. Dunk the sticky side of the marshmallows into the silver sanding sugar. Add these ears onto the cake. Stick the horn into the cake. Use the black buttercream to pipe the unicorn's eyes onto the front of the cake.

6. Decorate the mane with candy canes and snowflake candies. Sprinkle with silver and white sprinkles and slice to reveal the festive cake layers!

CHILI HOT CHOCOLATE CUPCAKES

MAKES 18 CUPCAKES

My first experience with chili hot chocolate was a bit shocking, because I wasn't expecting it so be so spicy! These cupcakes definitely pack a punch as well—they're made with a red velvet base and the frosting is good enough to eat by the spoonful! We're also filling the cupcakes with a surprise dark chocolate chili ganache, because it's the holidays and you deserve to indulge.

Cupcake Batter:

2½ cups cake flour
1 teaspoon salt
¼ cup cocoa powder
3 teaspoons chili powder
½ teaspoon cayenne pepper
1½ cups sugar
1½ cups vegetable oil
2 large eggs
¼ cup red food coloring
1 teaspoon vanilla extract
1 cup buttermilk
1½ teaspoons baking soda
2 teaspoons white vinegar

1 cup cocoa powder
3 teaspoons chili powder
½ teaspoon cayenne pepper
Cream Cheese Frosting (page 5)
Red and green food coloring
1 cup marzipan

Ganache Filling:

6 ounces semisweet chocolate, melted
¾ cup whipping cream
½ teaspoon chili powder

2 chili chocolate bars, broken into 18 pieces
54 mini marshmallows
Red sanding sugar

Bake the Cake:

1. Line 2 cupcake pans with paper liners, and preheat the oven to 350°F.

2. In a small bowl, whisk together the cake flour, salt, cocoa powder, chili powder, and cayenne pepper. Set aside.

3. Combine sugar and oil with an electric mixer, beating until well combined. Add the eggs and mix well. Add food coloring and vanilla and mix until combined. Add the flour mixture in 2 additions, alternating with the buttermilk. In a small bowl, combine the baking soda and vinegar, then add to the batter and mix to combine.

4. Divide the batter between your prepared pans. Bake for 15 to 20 minutes. Cool in the pan for 5 minutes, then turn out onto a wire rack and cool completely.

Frosting and Chili Peppers:

1. Combine the cocoa powder, chili powder, and cayenne pepper, then add to the frosting and mix for 2 to 3 minutes, or until light and fluffy. Place the frosting into a piping bag fitted with a #2D (large star/flower) piping tip.

2. Using 3 to 4 drops, dye ¾ of the marzipan red. Shape it into chile peppers.

3. Dye the remaining marzipan green with just a couple drops, and shape it into the stems. Stick them onto the chile peppers and set aside.

(Continued on page 55)

Make the Ganache:

1. Combine the semisweet chocolate with the whipping cream. Add the chili powder and mix well. Place in the fridge until thickened, but still liquid, about 30 minutes to an hour.

2. Use a knife or a small spoon to scoop out a ¾ inch -deep hole in the center of the cupcake and fill with the ganache.

Decorate the Cupcakes:

1. Pipe a swirl of frosting onto each cupcake. Stick a piece of chili chocolate into the top of the cupcake. Decorate with a marzipan chile pepper and 3 mini marshmallows.

2. Sprinkle with red sanding sugar and enjoy!

GINGERBREAD MAN CUPCAKES

MAKES 18 CUPCAKES

This cupcake recipe is so moist and flavorful. It tastes exactly like Christmas! They are great as muffins too, so if you don't want something too sweet, these are perfect without the frosting as well.

Cake Batter:
1 cup boiling water
2 teaspoons baking soda
2½ cups all-purpose flour
2 teaspoons ground ginger
1½ teaspoons ground cinnamon
½ teaspoon ground cloves
½ teaspoon ground nutmeg
½ teaspoon salt
½ cup unsalted butter, room
   temperature
⅔ cup brown sugar
1 cup molasses
⅓ cup ginger jam
2 eggs

Gingerbread Cookie Dough (page 183)
Yellow and brown food coloring
2 teaspoons Gingerbread Spice Mix (page 147)
Buttercream (page 11)
½ cup ginger jam
18 pieces of candied ginger
Gold sprinkles

Bake the Cupcakes:
1. Line a cupcake pan with paper liners and preheat the oven to 350°F.

2. Mix together the boiling water and baking soda. In a separate bowl, sift together the flour, spices, and salt.

3. Beat the butter with an electric mixer until pale and fluffy. Add the brown sugar and keep beating until fluffy. Add the molasses, baking soda mixture, flour mixture, and ginger jam. Add the eggs and beat until combined.

4. Divide the batter evenly into lined cupcake pans. Bake for 15 to 20 minutes until a skewer inserted into the cupcakes comes out clean. Transfer the cakes to a wire rack and cool completely.

Bake the Cookies:
1. Roll the dough out between 2 sheets of parchment paper.

2. Use a cookie stamp to cut out gingerbread man cookies. Place them on a baking sheet lined with parchment paper.

3. Bake at 350°F for 10 minutes, or until the edges are just starting to brown. Cool completely.

Assembly:
1. Add a couple drops of yellow and brown food coloring and the Gingerbread Spice Mix to your buttercream and beat to combine.

2. Place the buttercream into a piping bag fitted with a #2D (large star/flower) piping tip.

3. Cut a hole into the center of each of the cupcakes. Fill the hole with some ginger jam.

4. Pipe a swirl of buttercream on top of each cupcake. Decorate with gold sprinkles, a piece of candied ginger, and a gingerbread man.

CANDY CANE CUPCAKE-CAKE

MAKES 24 CUPCAKES

This is the perfect treat for a holiday party! We're using my classic vanilla cupcake recipe to create a fun pull-apart cupcake cake. Invite your guests to take a cupcake and pretty soon this candy cane will be nothing but a memory.

Cupcake Base:
1 cup unsalted butter, room temperature
2 cups sugar
3 teaspoons vanilla extract
6 large eggs
3 cups all-purpose flour
1 teaspoon baking soda
1 teaspoon salt
1½ cups sour cream

Buttercream:
4 cups unsalted butter, room temperature
2 teaspoons vanilla extract, or seeds from 1 vanilla bean
7½ cups confectioners' sugar
Red food coloring

Bake the Cupcakes:
1. Line 2 cupcake pans with paper liners and preheat the oven to 350°F.

2. Beat the butter and sugar with an electric mixer until pale and smooth. Add the vanilla extract and eggs one at a time, mixing with each addition.

3. In a separate bowl, combine the flour, baking soda, and salt. Add this to the batter in 2 additions, alternating with the sour cream.

4. Spoon the batter into your lined cupcake pans. Bake for 15 to 20 minutes, or until a skewer inserted into the centers comes out clean. Cool completely.

Make the Buttercream:
1. Beat the butter with an electric mixer until pale and fluffy. Add the vanilla extract and confectioners' sugar 1 cup at a time, beating with each addition.

2. Split between 2 bowls and dye half of the buttercream red using 4 to 5 drops of food coloring.

Assembly:
1. Arrange the cupcakes into the shape of a candy cane. Make sure that the candy cane is on the surface that you will be serving it on—it will be almost impossible to move it once decorated!

2. Place the white buttercream into a piping bag fitted with a #1A (large round) piping tip. Place the red buttercream into a piping bag fitted with a #8B (large star) piping tip.

3. Pipe squiggles of each color onto the candy cane. Enjoy!

Sugarplum Cupcakes

MAKE 18 CUPCAKES

If you are a fan of The Nutcracker, *these sweet cupcakes are for you! We're using a cool technique to feature two styles of buttercream and they feature some cute Sugarplum Truffles on top! If that wasn't enough, the cupcakes are filled with berry jam!*

Cake Batter:
1 cup unsalted butter, room temperature
2 cups sugar
3 teaspoons vanilla extract
6 large eggs
3 cups all-purpose flour
1 teaspoon baking soda
1 teaspoon salt
1½ cups sour cream
1 cup mixed berry jam

Buttercream:
3 cups unsalted butter, room temperature
2 teaspoons vanilla extract, or seeds from 1 vanilla bean
7 cups confectioners' sugar
Pink food coloring

⅓ cup purple sanding sugar
⅓ cup silver sprinkles
⅓ cup white sprinkles
18 Sugarplum Truffles (page 115)

Bake the Cake:

1. Line a cupcake pan with paper liners and preheat the oven to 350°F.

2. Beat the butter and sugar with an electric mixer until pale and smooth. Add the vanilla extract and eggs one at a time, mixing with each addition.

3. In a separate bowl, combine the flour, baking soda, and salt. Add this to the batter in 2 additions, alternating with the sour cream.

4. Spoon the batter into lined cupcake pans. Bake for 15 to 20 minutes, or until a skewer inserted into the centers comes out clean. Cool completely.

Make the Buttercream:

1. Beat the butter with an electric mixer until pale and fluffy. Add the vanilla extract and confectioners' sugar 1 cup at a time, beating with each addition.

2. Use a couple drops of food coloring to dye the buttercream pale pink. Place the buttercream in a piping bag fitted with a #4B (large open star) piping tip.

Assembly:

1. Cut a hole in the center of each cupcake and fill it with mixed berry jam.

2. Pipe a disk of buttercream onto the cupcakes. In a small bowl, combine the purple sanding sugar, silver sprinkles, and white sprinkles. Dunk the cupcakes into the sprinkle mixture, coating the entire disk of buttercream in the sprinkles.

3. Pipe some more buttercream onto the cupcake, but this time in a swirl pattern.

4. Top with a Sugarplum Truffle and enjoy!

CHRISTMAS CUPCAKES 5 WAYS

DECORATE AS MANY CUPCAKES AS YOU WANT—I RECOMMEND ONE OF EACH

These festive cupcakes are ready to celebrate the holidays with you! They are all quite easy to decorate, so they are perfect for beginners and experts alike!

Food coloring
Buttercream (page 11)
6 cupcakes (page 59)
Festive sprinkles and candies

Tree Cupcake:

1. Place some green buttercream into a piping bag fitted with a #2D (large star) piping tip.

2. Pipe a swirl onto the cupcake. Decorate with star sprinkles and a gumball at the top.

Santa Hat Cupcake:

1. Place some red buttercream in a piping bag fitted with a #2A (large round) piping tip. Place some white food coloring in a piping bag fitted with a #27 (small star) piping tip.

2. Pipe a swirl with the red buttercream. Pipe white dollops around the perimeter of the red swirl, as well as one dollop on the top.

(Continued on next page)

Christmas Light Cupcake:

1. Place some white buttercream into a piping bag fitted with a #2A (large round) piping tip. Place some black buttercream into a piping bag fitted with a #4 (small round) piping tip.

2. Pipe a swirl of white buttercream onto the cupcake. Pipe a "string" of black buttercream in the crevice of the white buttercream.

3. Stick some Christmas light–shaped candies, or halved M&M's, onto the cupcake to look like Christmas lights.

Wreath Cupcake:

1. Place some green buttercream into a piping bag fitted with a #27 (small star) piping tip. Place some red buttercream into a piping bag fitted with a small, round piping tip.

2. Cover the surface of the cupcake with some white buttercream. Draw a circle in the buttercream with any pointy utensil, to use as a guide. Pipe dollops of the green buttercream along the circle, then repeat, but piping on top of the original dollops, to give the wreath some depth.

3. Decorate with colorful candies. Draw a ribbon on the top of the wreath with the red buttercream.

Peppermint Swirl Cupcake:

1. Spread or pipe a vertical line of red buttercream into a piping bag fitted with a #2A (large round) piping tip. Fill the rest of the bag with white buttercream and squeeze everything down toward the tip—be sure to include a couple teaspoons of peppermint extract for this one.

2. Pipe a swirl onto the cupcake to reveal a red and white swirl!

Santa Cupcakes

These marble cupcakes are perfect for a holiday bake sale or weekend baking with your family at home!

Cupcake Batter:
1 cup all-purpose flour
1¾ teaspoons baking powder
¼ teaspoon salt
¼ cup unsalted butter, room
    temperature
½ cup granulated sugar
½ teaspoon vanilla extract
1 large egg
½ cup milk
Red food coloring

Buttercream:
1 cup unsalted butter, room
    temperature
½ teaspoon vanilla extract
2½ cups confectioners' sugar
Peach and red food coloring
Chocolate chips
Red Smarties or M&M's

Bake the Cupcakes:

1. Line a cupcake pan with paper liners and preheat the oven to 350°F.

2. Combine the flour, baking powder, and salt in a bowl. In a separate bowl, beat the butter and sugar with an electric mixer until pale and fluffy. Add the vanilla extract and egg and mix to combine. Add the dry ingredients in 2 additions, alternating with the milk. Divide the batter in half and dye one half red (about 3 drops).

3. Fill the cupcake pan halfway with the red batter, then fill the pan the rest of the way with the white batter. Gently swirl the colors together with a knife. Bake for 15 to 18 minutes, until fully cooked. Cool completely.

Make the Buttercream:

1. Cream the butter with an electric mixer until pale and fluffy. Add the vanilla extract and beat until combined. Add the confectioners' sugar 1 cup at a time and beat for 3 to 5 minutes, until fluffy.

2. Divide the buttercream into 3 bowls and use 1 drop to dye a bowl peach, 3 drops to dye one red, and leave the remaining white. Place the white buttercream in a piping bag fitted with a #2A (large round) piping tip.

To Decorate:

1. Spread an even layer of peach buttercream onto each cupcake and smooth the surface. Smooth some red buttercream to create the hat portion. Pipe a large white dollop for the pompom of the hat and small white dollops around the rim of the hat. Pipe more dollops to create his beard.

2. Stick 2 chocolate chips on the cupcake as the eyes and a red Smarties or M&M for the nose. Enjoy!

Christmas Bauble Cakelettes

MAKES 6-8 CAKELETTES

These pretty little ornaments are essentially jumbo cake pops. They are coated in a beautiful metallic chocolate coating and will look very at home on your holiday dessert plate! Looking to spice things up? Add some chocolate chips, orange zest, or other flavorings to the cake pop mix!

1 cup unsalted butter, room temperature
2 cups sugar
3 teaspoons vanilla extract
6 large eggs
3 cups all-purpose flour
1 teaspoon baking soda
1 teaspoon salt
1½ cups sour cream
Buttercream (page 11)
4 cups white candy melts, melted
Mini chocolate peanut butter cups
Silver, gold, and pink metallic food spray
Metallic sprinkles

Bake the Cake:

1. Preheat the oven to 350°F. Beat the butter and sugar with an electric mixer until pale and smooth. Add the vanilla and eggs one at a time, mixing with each addition.

2. In a separate bowl, combine the flour, baking soda, and salt. Add this to the batter in 2 additions, alternating with the sour cream.

3. Spoon the batter into 2 greased cupcake pans. Bake for 15 to 20 minutes, or until a skewer inserted into the centers comes out clean. Cool completely.

Assemble and Decorate Cakelettes:

1. Crumble the cupcakes into a bowl. Add about 2 cups of buttercream and mix with an electric mixer, until the cake is broken into fine crumbs and can be shaped.

2. Shape the cake mixture into 6 to 8 balls and place on a plate lined with plastic wrap. Place in the fridge to chill for 1 hour, or until firm.

3. Once the cakes are firm, roll them in your hands to shape them into even smoother balls and flatten any lumps. Return to the fridge to chill for 30 minutes.

4. Dunk each ball into the melted white candy and fully submerge. Remove with a fork and allow the excess to drip off. Place on a plate lined with plastic wrap and return to the fridge for 30 minutes, or until the candy melts have hardened.

5. Place the peanut butter cups on a sheet of parchment paper, with the widest side facing down. Spray all sides with silver food spray. Set aside. Place the cakelettes on a sheet of parchment paper and spray with either the gold, silver, or pink food spray. Allow to dry at room temperature for 10 to 15 minutes.

6. Stick the bottom of the peanut butter cups in some remaining white candy melts and attach one to each cakelette.

7. Then decorate the cakelettes with sprinkles, using small amounts of white candy melts as glue. Enjoy!

Evergreen Shortbread Cookies, page 101

COOKIES

3D Reindeer Cookies

MAKES ABOUT 6 REINDEER

These adorable cookies are the cutest addition to your holiday baking! The best part is that they don't require any specialty cookie cutter! Use your favorite reindeer cookie cutter and follow along to make them 3D.

Cookie Dough:
2 cups all-purpose flour
2 teaspoon ground ginger
1 teaspoon ground cinnamon
½ teaspoon ground nutmeg
¼ teaspoon cloves
¼ teaspoon baking soda
¼ teaspoon salt
½ cup unsalted butter, room temperature
⅓ cup brown sugar
⅓ cup molasses
1 large egg

Royal Icing (page 99)
Brown and red food coloring
Gold and black round sprinkles

Make the Cookies:

1. Combine the flour, ginger, cinnamon, nutmeg, cloves, baking soda, and salt. Set aside.

2. Beat the butter and brown sugar with an electric mixer until smooth. Add the molasses and egg and mix until combined. Add the dry ingredients and mix until just combined. Divide the dough in 2 and wrap each half in plastic wrap.

3. Refrigerate for 1 hour, until firm.

4. Preheat the oven to 350°F. Roll the dough out on a floured surface until it is ⅛ inch thick.

5. To create the 3D cookies, use a reindeer cookie cutter to cut out just the body of the reindeer. Cut little notches into the body, where the legs are meant to be. For the legs, cut an H-shape into the dough, making sure the H is twice as wide as the thickness of the cookie dough. This will ensure that the body will fit into the legs. You will need 2 H-cookies per body.

6. Bake the cookies for about 10 minutes, until the edges begin to darken. Transfer the cookies to a wire rack and cool completely.

Decoration & Assembly:

1. Using just 1 drop of food coloring, dye half of the icing light brown. Divide the remaining icing in half. Use 2 drops food coloring to dye one half dark brown. Divide the remaining icing in half again and use 1 drop

(Continued on next page)

to dye half red, leaving the remaining half white. Place all the icing in piping bags fitted with small, round piping tips.

2. Lay the cookies on a flat surface. Use the light brown icing to create the reindeer's fur, both on the body and the leg cookies. Place the round black sprinkles onto the face as the reindeer's eyes. Allow the icing to dry completely, 1 to 2 hours.

3. Use the dark brown icing to create the antlers, hooves, and noses, for non-Rudolph reindeer. Use the red icing for the collars and immediately place the round gold sprinkles on top. These will look like jingle bells! For Rudolph, also use the red icing for the nose. Use the white icing for the spots, tail, and tummy. Allow the icing to dry completely, about 1 hour.

4. To assemble, place the notches in the body cookies into the H-slots in the legs. Enjoy!

Festive Christmas Macarons

MAKES ABOUT 1 DOZEN MACARONS

Macarons have a reputation of being difficult to make, but this recipe is foolproof! These sweet little macarons are ready for the holidays and will be in your kitchen in no time, even if you're a beginner.

Macarons:
1 cup confectioners' sugar
¾ cup almond flour (not almond meal)
2 large egg whites
Pinch of cream of tartar
¼ cup superfine sugar
1 teaspoon vanilla extract
Green, red, brown, and orange food
    coloring

Ganache Filling:
4 ounces milk chocolate, melted
¼ cup whipping cream, hot
½ teaspoon peppermint extract

Festive sprinkles
Edible ink pens
Candies for decoration

Make the Macarons:

1. Prepare a baking sheet lined with parchment paper or a Silpat mat.

2. Combine the confectioners' sugar and almond flour in a bowl, then sift 3 times.

3. Place the egg whites in a large bowl and beat with an electric mixer until foamy. Add the cream of tartar, then beat until soft peaks form. Add the superfine sugar and beat on high speed until stiff peaks form. Add the vanilla extract and gently mix to combine. Sift the dry mixture into the egg mixture and gently fold to combine.

4. Divide the mixture into 5 bowls and, using a couple drops each, dye one each green, red, brown, and pale orange/peach, leaving the remaining bowl white. Place each color of macaron batter into individual piping bags fitted with medium-sized round piping tips.

5. Pipe the macarons into Santa, present, candy cane, gingerbread, snowman, and reindeer shapes onto your prepared baking sheet. Be sure to make at least 2 of each shape, as the macaron will need a top and a bottom.

6. Tap the baking sheet on your work surface several times to remove any air bubbles. Allow the macarons to sit at room temperature for 30 minutes. Set the oven to 375°F and heat for 5 minutes, then reduce to 325°F.

(Continued on page 77)

Place the macarons in the oven once you've lowered the temperature, and bake for 6 to 8 minutes, rotating the baking sheet halfway through baking time.

7. Allow the macarons to cool completely on the baking sheet.

Make the Filling:

1. Combine the melted milk chocolate, whipping cream, and peppermint extract in a bowl. Place in the fridge until set, about 1 hour.

2. Beat the ganache with an electric mixer until it lightens in color and reaches stiff peaks. Place it in a piping bag fitted with a round piping tip.

Assembly:

1. Use edible ink pens and candies to decorate half of the macarons (the top halves), using extra ganache to attach the candies.

2. Pipe the filling onto the bottom half of the macarons and place the matching half on top.

3. Roll the sides of the macarons into festive sprinkles. Enjoy!

Peppermint Hot Chocolate Cookies

MAKES 1 DOZEN COOKIES

This is my favorite cookie recipe because it tastes like a mix between brownies and cookies. We're taking them to another level by adding more chocolate and a toasted marshmallow on top! I challenge you to eat just one!

½ cup unsalted butter, melted
12 ounces dark chocolate, melted
1¾ cups all-purpose flour
1½ teaspoons baking powder
¼ teaspoon salt
¼ cup cocoa powder
1¼ cups brown sugar
3 large eggs
1 teaspoon vanilla extract
1 teaspoon peppermint extract
½ cup crushed candy canes
1 large peppermint chocolate bar, broken
   into pieces
12 large marshmallows, sliced in half

1. Whisk together the melted butter and chocolate in a bowl. Set aside.

2. In a separate bowl, combine the flour, baking powder, salt, and cocoa powder.

3. In a large bowl, beat the brown sugar, eggs, and vanilla and peppermint extracts, with an electric mixer. Add the butter and chocolate mixture and mix until combined. Add the dry ingredients and mix until just combined.

4. Cover the bowl with plastic wrap and chill for 1 to 2 hours, or until the dough is firm.

5. Line a baking sheet with parchment paper and preheat the oven to 325°F. Once chilled, use an ice cream scooper to scoop out balls of dough and place them onto your prepared baking sheet, spacing them about 1 to 2 inches apart. Sprinkle some crushed candy canes on top. Bake for 8 to 10 minutes, or until the cookies begin to crack.

6. Remove the cookies from the oven and place a piece of chocolate on top of each cookie. Sprinkle more crushed candy canes on top, then top with a marshmallow half. Return to the oven and bake for 3 to 4 more minutes.

7. Allow the cookies to cool until warm and enjoy!

CHRISTMAS SWIRL COOKIES

MAKES 2 DOZEN COOKIES

This recipe is a twist on my Rainbow Spiral Cookies from my first cookbook, Unicorn Food! *This is a delicious and easy-to-make sugar cookie dough and they look wonderfully festive with a red and green swirl. To make them extra special, roll the log of dough in sprinkles before slicing and baking.*

½ cup granulated sugar

2 tablespoons confectioners' sugar

¼ teaspoon salt

1 egg

1 teaspoon vanilla extract

1 cup unsalted butter, room temperature

2 cups all-purpose flour

Red and green food coloring

1. Combine the granulated sugar, confectioners' sugar, and salt in a bowl. In a separate bowl, combine the egg and vanilla extract. Set both bowls aside.

2. Beat the butter with an electric mixer until pale and fluffy. Add the sugar mixture and mix until combined. Add the egg mixture and combine. Gradually add the flour and mix until just combined.

3. Divide the dough into 3 balls. Using about 3 drops of each food coloring, dye one ball red, one ball green, and leave the remaining ball white.

4. Sandwich the white dough between 2 sheets of floured parchment paper and roll out into a 10x12-inch rectangle. Set aside. Repeat with the red and green dough, rolling them out separately.

5. Remove the top sheets of parchment paper from the beige and green dough, and flip the green dough on top. Then remove the remaining sheet of parchment paper from the green dough and the top sheet from the red dough. Flip the red dough on top of the green dough. Keep the parchment paper on top of the red dough and roll a rolling pin over it several times to seal all 3 layers together.

6. Remove the top sheet of parchment paper and trim the edges of the dough to create a clean rectangle shape. Position the dough with the long edge facing you and roll the dough away from you, into a spiral. Roll the dough log tightly in plastic wrap and place in the freezer for 1 hour.

7. Line a baking sheet with parchment paper and preheat the oven to 325°F. Slice the chilled dough into ¼-inch-thick slices and place on your prepared baking sheet. Bake for 14 minutes, until the edges are just slightly golden. Cool completely and enjoy!

Woven Stocking Cookies

MAKES 9-10 COOKIES

This is a very fun cookie technique that will have people guessing how you did it! No stocking cookie cutter? A mitten or hat shape would be just as cute!

½ cup granulated sugar
2 tablespoons confectioners' sugar
1 teaspoon Gingerbread Spice Mix
   (page 147)
¼ teaspoon salt
1 egg
1 teaspoon vanilla extract
1 cup unsalted butter, room
   temperature
2 cups all-purpose flour
Red and green food coloring
½ cup white chocolate, melted
1 cup sweetened coconut flakes
¼ cup holly sprinkles

Bake the Cookies:

1. Line a baking sheet with parchment paper and preheat the oven to 325°F.

2. Combine the granulated sugar, confectioners' sugar, Gingerbread Spice Mix, and salt in a bowl. In a separate bowl, combine the egg and vanilla extract. Set both bowls aside.

3. Beat the butter with an electric mixer until pale and fluffy. Add the sugar mixture and mix until combined. Add the egg mixture and combine. Gradually add the flour and mix until just combined.

4. Divide the dough into 2 balls. Using about 3 drops of each food coloring, dye one ball red and the other green.

5. Sandwich the green dough between 2 sheets of parchment paper and roll it into a 9x9-inch square. Trim off the edges to create a clean square, then slice it into ½-inch-wide strips. Repeat with the red dough.

6. Weave the red and green dough together in a basket-weave style. Don't worry if the dough breaks; simply press it together with your fingers. All tears will be hidden in the baking process. Once you have woven all the dough together, don't press down on it—everything is woven and secure.

7. Use a stocking cookie cutter to cut out cookies. Gently transfer them to your prepared baking sheet.

8. Bake for 14 minutes, or until the edges are just starting to brown. Cool completely.

Decorate the Cookies:

1. Spread some white chocolate onto the top of the stocking cookies. Dunk the cookies into sweetened coconut flakes to make them look fluffy!

2. Add another dollop of white chocolate to the stocking and use it as glue to attach some holly sprinkles.

3. Place the cookies in the fridge for the white chocolate to set, about 30 minutes. Then enjoy!

CABLE KNIT MITTEN COOKIES

Knitted mitten are so cozy during colder weather, just like these cookies! If you'd like to go all out, check out the Cable Knit Cake on page 11.

Sugar Cookie Dough:
2 cups flour
¼ teaspoon salt
½ teaspoon baking powder
½ cup unsalted butter
1 cup sugar
2 tablespoons milk
1 egg
½ teaspoon vanilla extract

Royal Icing (page 99)
White edible glitter

Bake the Cookies:

1. Mix together the flour, salt. and baking powder in a bowl. In a separate bowl, cream the butter and sugar with an electric mixer until it becomes light and fluffy. Add the milk, egg, and vanilla, and mix well. Then slowly add the flour mixture until it is just combined.

2. Shape the dough into a ball, wrap it in plastic wrap, and place in the refrigerator for 1 hour.

3. Line a baking sheet with parchment paper and preheat the oven to 350°F. Roll out the chilled cookie dough onto a lightly floured surface until it is ¼ inch thick. Then using a mitten-shaped cookie cutter (or a knife), cut out mitten-shaped cookies. Place them onto your prepared baking sheet, and bake for about 10 minutes, until they're lightly golden.

4. Transfer the cookies to a cooling rack and allow them to fully cool.

To Decorate:

1. Place the icing into a piping bag fitted with a round tip, and draw a line around the perimeter of each cookie, as well as a line across the cuff of the mittens.

2. Add about 2 teaspoons of water to half of the icing, to give it a thinner consistency. Fill the larger part of the mittens with this runny icing and allow it to fully set, about 1 hour.

3. Fill in the cuff area with the runny icing and sprinkle the white glitter on top. Allow this to set for about 30 minutes, then tap the cookies to remove any excess glitter.

4. Using the thicker icing, pipe a cable knit pattern onto the cookies. Refer to the techniques on page 13 if you need some ideas. Allow this to fully set, about 1 hour, then enjoy!

Nordic Winter Mitten Cookies

MAKES 1 DOZEN COOKIES

These sweet cookies were originally designed after my favorite hat and scarf set. I love to incorporate pink into the holidays, as it's a refreshing change from the classic holiday red.

1 batch Sugar Cookie Dough (page 85)
Royal Icing (page 99)
Bright pink food coloring
Gold luster dust

Bake the Cookies:

1. Line a baking sheet with parchment paper and preheat the oven to 350°F.

2. Roll out the cookie dough onto a lightly floured surface until it is ¼ inch thick. Use a cookie cutter to cut out mitten-shaped cookies. Place them onto your prepared baking sheet and bake for about 10 minutes, until they're lightly golden.

3. Transfer the cookies to a cooling rack and allow them to fully cool.

To Decorate:

1. Place about ⅓ of the icing in a separate bowl, and dye it bright pink. Leave the remaining icing white.

2. Using a piping bag fitted with a #4 (small round) piping tip, pipe an outline around the mitten cookies with the white icing. Allow this to fully set, about 20 minutes. Then add 1 to 2 teaspoons of water to the white icing until it becomes slightly runnier. Fill in the cookies with the runny white icing, and allow this to fully set as well, about 20 to 30 minutes.

3. Place the pink icing in a piping bag fitted with a #2 (very small, round) piping tip, and pipe a Nordic design onto the cookies.

4. With a small brush, dust the gold luster dust onto the cuff of the mittens to create a golden cuff. Allow the pink icing to fully set for another 20 minutes or so, and you're done!

PLAID MITTEN COOKIES

MAKES 1 DOZEN COOKIES

Snuggle under a blanket with a plate of plaid cookies and a cup of hot cocoa!

1 batch Sugar Cookie Dough (page 85)
Royal Icing (page 99)
Food coloring

Bake the Cookies:
1. Line a baking sheet with parchment paper and preheat the oven to 350°F. Roll the cookie dough out until ¼ inch thick and use a cookie cutter to cut out mitten shapes. Transfer to your prepared baking sheet and bake for 10 minutes, or until the edges are just starting to brown. Transfer to a wire rack and cool completely.

Decorate the Cookies:
1. Divide the icing into as many bowls as colors you'd like—each mitten uses 3 shades of icing. Add ¼ teaspoon of water to the icing that you are going to use as the base (the background color) of the mittens. Place all shades of icing into piping bags fitted with #2 (small round) piping tips.

2. Using your base icing, pipe a border of icing around the perimeter of the cookies and fill in the border with the icing. Allow the icing to harden completely, about 1 hour. Using the icing for the accent color of the plaid pattern, pipe a large checkered pattern (vertical and horizontal lines) onto the cookies. Use the remaining icing color to add 3 more stripes to each stripe you've already piped on (both vertically and horizontally). If you're running out of room, just add 2 stripes.

3. Allow the icing to fully harden, about 1 hour. Enjoy your cozy cookies!

CANDY CANE SUGAR COOKIES

MAKES ABOUT 1 DOZEN COOKIES

This is my favorite sugar cookie recipe of all time! The dough has a gentle sweetness to it and is so easy to work with. This is a perfect recipe to make with young children because of how fun it is to twist the dough together and shape it into candy canes!

2 cups flour
¼ teaspoon salt
½ teaspoon baking powder
½ cup unsalted butter
1 cup sugar
2 tablespoons milk
1 egg
1 teaspoon peppermint extract
½ teaspoon vanilla extract
Red food coloring
½ teaspoon matcha green tea powder

1. Line a baking sheet with parchment paper and preheat the oven to 350°F.

2. Mix together the flour, salt, and baking powder in a bowl. In a separate bowl, cream the butter and sugar with an electric mixer until it becomes light and fluffy. Add the milk, egg, peppermint, and vanilla extract, and mix well. Then slowly add the flour mixture and mix until it is just combined.

3. Shape the dough into a ball, then divide into 3 pieces. Leave one ball white, dye one red with a couple drops of food coloring, and the other green with the matcha.

4. Lightly dust some flour onto your countertop. Pull off a piece of dough from each ball and roll the dough out into a 5 to 6 inch–long log. Twirl all the colors together, then bend to create a candy cane shape. Trim off the uneven ends with a sharp knife.

5. Place them onto your prepared baking sheet, and bake for about 9 minutes, until lightly golden. Transfer the cookies to cooling racks and allow to fully cool.

CHRISTMAS BEAR EDIBLE TREE DECORATIONS

MAKES ABOUT 1 DOZEN COOKIES

Decorating the tree is one of my favorite Christmas traditions, and it's even better when I can decorate it with cookies! These little bears are so precious and if stored carefully, can last you year after year!

Gingerbread Cookie Dough (page 183)
Royal Icing (page 99)
Food coloring of choice
Holly sprinkles or your desired decorations
String

Make the Cookies:

1. Preheat the oven to 350°F. Place the dough on a sheet of floured parchment paper and roll out to ⅛ inch thick. Use a bear cookie cutter to cut out shapes. Use a small straw or a skewer to make one hole in each cookie.

2. Bake the cookies for about 10 minutes, until the edges begin to darken. Transfer the baking sheets to a wire rack and stick the straw or skewer back through the holes, in case any have gotten smaller while baking. Allow the cookies to cool completely.

To Decorate:

1. Dye the icing your desired shades of colors.

2. Place the icing in piping bags fitted with round piping tips and pipe the bears' facial features as well as any festive clothing you'd like them to be wearing. To make a furry scarf, pour the icing into a piping bag fitted with a #17 (small star) piping tip. Decorate with sprinkles as you like! Allow the icing to dry completely, 2 hours or overnight.

3. Feed some string through the holes in the cookies and tie at the ends. Hang these on your Christmas tree and enjoy!

Reindeer Food Shortbread Cookies

MAKES ABOUT 2 CUPS OF TINY COOKIES

This shortbread recipe has the perfect, tiniest touch of salt, which makes these cookies absolutely delectable. Leave these cookies out for Santa's reindeer on Christmas Eve, and I'm sure you'll see some extra presents under the tree!

1 cup unsalted butter, room temperature
½ cup confectioners' sugar
1 teaspoon vanilla extract
2 cups all-purpose flour
½ teaspoon salt
1 tablespoon each red and green sprinkles
½ cup white chocolate, melted

1. Beat the butter with an electric mixer until pale and fluffy. Add the confectioners' sugar and beat for 2 minutes, until well combined. Add the vanilla and combine.

2. In a separate bowl, combine the flour and salt. Add the butter mixture and red and green sprinkles and mix until the dough sticks together when pinched. Shape into a ball, wrap in plastic wrap, and chill in the fridge until firm, about 1 hour.

3. Line a baking sheet with parchment paper and preheat the oven to 325°F. Roll the chilled dough out on a floured surface to ¼ inch thick. Cut into ¾-inch squares.

4. Place on your prepared baking sheet and bake for 6 minutes, until the edges are just starting to brown. Cool on the pan completely.

5. Drizzle the white chocolate on top of the cookies and allow the chocolate to set, about 30 minutes.

CHRISTMAS TREE COOKIE STACK

This is a show-stopping cookie recipe! The quantities may seem overwhelming, but this is definitely a recipe for a crowd. You will need 10 star cookie cutters in graduated sizes from small to large, then get ready for some cookie construction!

Cookie Dough:

8 cups flour

1 teaspoon salt

2 teaspoons baking powder

2 tablespoons Gingerbread Spice Mix (page 147)

2 cups unsalted butter

4 cups sugar

½ cup milk

4 eggs

2 teaspoons vanilla extract

Royal Icing:

4 pounds confectioners' sugar

1 cup + 3 tablespoons meringue powder

1 cup cold water

½ cup wintry sprinkles

2 candy snowflakes

Bake the Cookies:

1. Mix together the flour, salt, baking powder, and Gingerbread Spice Mix in a bowl. In a separate bowl, cream the butter and sugar with an electric mixer until the mixture becomes light and fluffy. Add the milk, eggs, and vanilla, and mix well. Then slowly add the flour mixture until it is just combined.

2. Shape the dough into 4 balls, wrap each in plastic wrap, and place in the refrigerator for 1 hour.

3. Line baking sheets with parchment paper and preheat oven to 350°F. Lightly dust some flour onto your countertop, and working with one ball at a time, roll the dough out until it is ¼ inch thick. To make a tree, you'll need 10 star cookie cutters in graduated sizes from small to large. Cut out 2 cookies per cookie cutter. You'll need to use all 4 balls of dough.

4. Place cookies on your prepared baking sheets. Bake for about 10 minutes, until lightly golden. Transfer to cooling racks and allow to fully cool.

Make the Royal Icing:

1. Combine the confectioners' sugar and meringue powder in a large bowl. Add the cold water and beat for 7 minutes, until it is smooth and when drizzled, stays on the surface for a few seconds. Pour the icing into a piping bag fitted with a small, round piping tip.

Assembly:

1. Stack the cookies in graduated sizes from large to small. Pipe a small amount of icing between each layer to secure the cookies together.

2. Once the cookie tree has been built, pipe the icing onto the extending triangles. Sprinkle some wintry sprinkles on top. Top with 2 candy snowflakes and enjoy!

Spiced Holiday Woodland Sugar Cookies

MAKES 10-12 COOKIES

These are sugar cookies with a delicious, holiday citrus twist! I think that woodland creatures are so cute during the holidays and are a fun alternative to the classic Christmas cookie shapes.

Cookie Dough:
2 cups all-purpose flour
¼ teaspoon salt
½ teaspoon baking powder
1 teaspoon cinnamon
½ teaspoon ginger
¼ teaspoon nutmeg
¼ teaspoon ground cloves
¼ teaspoon allspice
½ cup unsalted butter
1 cup sugar
2 tablespoons milk
1 egg
½ teaspoon vanilla extract
1 teaspoon freshly grated orange zest

Royal Icing:
½ pound confectioners' sugar
2½ tablespoons meringue powder
Scant ¼ cup water
Food coloring

Bake the Cookies:
1. Mix together the flour, salt, baking powder, cinnamon, ginger, nutmeg, cloves, and allspice in a bowl. In a separate bowl, cream the butter and sugar with an electric mixer until it becomes light and fluffy. Add the milk to the mixture along with the egg, vanilla, and orange zest and mix well. Then slowly add the flour mixture until it is just combined.

2. Shape the dough into a ball, then divide into 2 balls. Wrap each in plastic wrap. Place them in the refrigerator to chill for 1 hour.

3. Line a baking sheet with parchment paper and preheat the oven to 350°F. Lightly dust some flour onto your countertop and roll the chilled dough out until it is ¼ inch thick. Cut out your desired shapes with cookie cutters. Place these onto your prepared baking sheet and bake for about 10 minutes, until lightly golden. Transfer to cooling racks and allow to fully cool.

Make the Icing:
1. Place the confectioners' sugar, meringue powder, and water into a bowl and beat with an electric mixer for about 7 minutes until the mixture is smooth and, when drizzled, stays on the surface for a few seconds. If you find that the icing is too thick, gradually add a few more drops of water.

2. Divide the icing into as many bowls as you like and dye it your desired colors. Place the icing into piping bags fitted with #4 (small round) piping tips.

Decorate the Cookies:
1. Work from the base color upward by piping a border of icing around the perimeter of the cookies. Fill in the cookie with the same color of icing and allow this layer to fully harden. Repeat the process with one color at a time, allowing the icing to fully set between each layer.

2. Once the cookies are decorated, allow the icing to fully set and enjoy!

Evergreen Shortbread Cookies

MAKES ABOUT 2 DOZEN COOKIES

Shortbread cookies are one of my favorite cookies, and this recipe is the best ever! This is a cute technique to add a festive touch to your cookies. I used a cookie stamp to create the tree shapes, but if you don't have access to one, simply use a cookie cutter and make the indentations with the end of a chopstick!

1 cup unsalted butter, room
    temperature
½ cup confectioners' sugar
1 teaspoon vanilla extract
2 cups all-purpose flour
¾ teaspoon salt
Green food coloring

1. Line a baking sheet with parchment paper and preheat the oven to 325°F.

2. Beat the butter with an electric mixer until pale and fluffy. Add the confectioners' sugar and beat for 2 minutes, until well combined. Add the vanilla and combine. In a separate bowl, combine the flour and salt, then add to the butter mixture. Mix until the dough sticks together when pinched.

3. Set aside ¼ of dough. Dye the remaining dough pale green (use just a drop or two of food coloring). Set aside ⅓ of the pale green dough. Add a few more drops of green food coloring to the dough and knead together. Set aside ½ of this dough. Add a few more drops of green food coloring to the remaining dough and knead.

4. Roll each ball of dough into a long log and arrange in an ombre pattern on a floured surface. Ideally, you want each tube of dough to be smaller than the size of your cookie cutter, so that multiple colors will be included in each cookie. If your work surface is too small, cut the logs in half lengthwise and continue the ombre pattern below.

5. Cover with a sheet of parchment paper. Roll a rolling pin on top to smooth the dough and blend all the colors together. Use a tree-shaped cookie cutter or pie stamper to cut out trees. Place them onto your prepared baking sheet.

6. Bake for 10 minutes, or until the edges are just starting to brown. Cool on the pan for 10 minutes, then transfer to a wire rack and cool completely. Enjoy!

Molasses Cookies

These cookies are my guilty pleasure when I want to have a treat with my morning coffee. They are delightfully chewy and the warmth of the ginger always makes me feel cozy inside.

¾ cup margarine, melted
1½ cups granulated sugar, divided
1 large egg
¼ cup molasses
2 cups all–purpose flour
2 teaspoons baking soda
½ teaspoon salt
1 teaspoon ground cinnamon
½ teaspoon ground cloves
½ teaspoon ground ginger
½ cup dark chocolate, melted
½ cup white chocolate, melted
Festive sprinkles

1. Place the margarine, 1 cup granulated sugar, and egg into a bowl and mix until smooth. Add the molasses and mix to combine.

2. In a separate bowl, combine the flour, baking soda, salt, cinnamon, cloves, and ginger. Add this to the sugar mixture and mix until combined. Cover the bowl with plastic wrap and chill in the fridge for 1 hour, or, if you need to, overnight.

3. Line a baking sheet with parchment paper and preheat the oven to 375°F. Roll the chilled dough into 1½ tablespoon-sized balls, then roll them into the remaining ½ cup granulated sugar. Place on a baking sheet lined with parchment paper and space them about 1 inch apart.

4. Bake for 6 to 9 minutes, until the tops are cracked. Cool completely.

5. Dunk the cookies halfway into the dark or white chocolate and decorate with festive sprinkles. Enjoy!

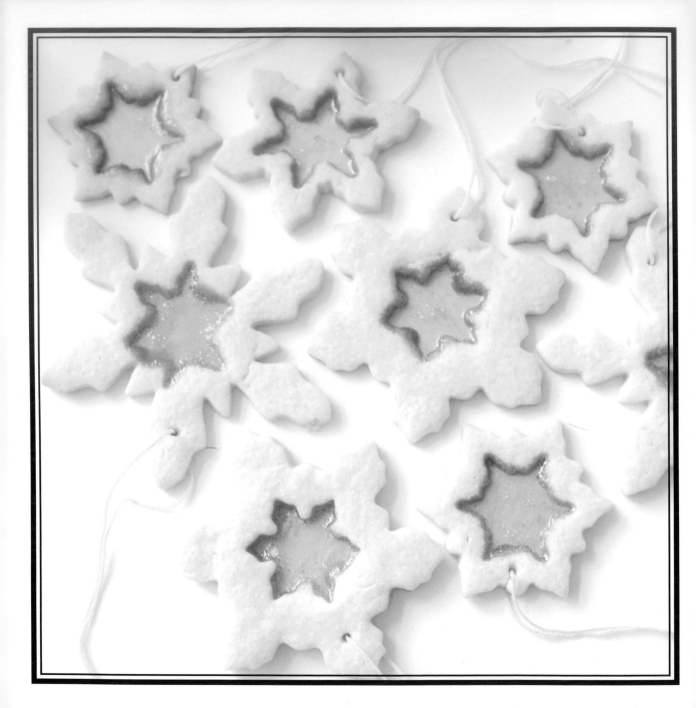

Snowflake Window Cookies

**SERVING SIZE WILL DEPEND ON THE SIZE OF YOUR COOKIE CUTTER;
ROUGHLY 6-10 COOKIES**

These beautiful cookies look best when hung in your windows! If you are hesitant to make the hard candy from scratch, any hard candy or lollipop can be substituted.

Candy Center:
1¼ cups granulated
   sugar
½ cup water
¾ cup light corn syrup
Blue food coloring

1 batch Sugar Cookie
   Dough (page 85)
String

Make the Candies:

1. Combine the sugar, water, and corn syrup in a deep pot over medium heat. Increase the heat to high and attach a candy thermometer to the pot. When the temperature reaches 300°F, add a drop of blue food coloring and mix until fully combined. Bring the heat up to 310°F, then remove from the heat and stir with a rubber spatula until it stops bubbling.

2. Pour the mixture into a silicone mold and cool at room temperature, until hardened. Unmold the candy and set aside.

Make the Cookies:

1. Prepare a baking sheet lined with parchment paper and preheat the oven to 350°F. Roll the dough out on a floured surface until it is ¼ inch thick. Cut out snowflake shapes and place them on your prepared baking sheet. Use a smaller snowflake cookie cutter to cut out centers from the cookies.

2. Place the hardened candy in a freezer bag and crush them into large chunks. Place some candy into the center of each cookies—don't add too much or too little (it may take some trial and error to gauge how much you need, so I recommend making a test batch of 3 cookies, placing a different amount of candy in the center of each). Poke little holes at the tops of the cookies with a lollipop stick.

3. Bake for 10 minutes, until the cookies are just starting to brown around the edges and the candy center has melted. Allow these to cool completely on the baking sheet.

4. Once fully cooled, thread some string through the holes of the cookies and hang them by the window so that the sun can shine through the beautiful candy center!

Sugar Cookie Gift Tags

MAKES 1 DOZEN COOKIES

Add an extra special touch to your gift wrapping this year! Use edible ink pens to write your recipient's name on the cookie, wrap it in cellophane, and attach it to your gift.

Cookie Dough:
2 cups flour
¼ teaspoon salt
½ teaspoon baking powder
2 teaspoons Gingerbread Spice Mix
   (page 147)
½ cup unsalted butter
1 cup sugar
2 tablespoons milk
1 egg
½ teaspoon vanilla extract

Royal Icing:
1 pound confectioners' sugar
5 tablespoons meringue powder
¼ cup cold water
Icing decorations
Edible ink pens

Bake the Cookies:
1. Mix together the flour, salt, baking powder, and Gingerbread Spice Mix in a bowl. In a separate bowl, cream the butter and sugar with an electric mixer until it becomes light and fluffy. Add the milk, egg, and vanilla, and mix well. Then slowly add the flour mixture until it is just combined.

2. Shape the dough into a ball, wrap it in plastic wrap, and place in the refrigerator for 1 hour.

3. Line a baking sheet with parchment paper and preheat the oven to 350°F. Lightly dust some flour onto your countertop, and roll the dough out until it is ¼ inch thick. Cut out shapes with your desired cookie cutters. If you plan on feeding ribbon through the cookies, poke holes in the cookies. Place them on your prepared baking sheet, and bake for about 10 minutes, until lightly golden. Transfer the cookies to cooling racks and allow to fully cool.

Make the Royal Icing:
1. Combine the confectioners' sugar and meringue powder in a large bowl. Add the water and beat for 7 minutes, until it is smooth and, when drizzled, stays on the surface for a few seconds.

2. Pour the icing into a piping bag fitted with a small, round piping tip.

To Decorate:
1. Pipe a border of icing along the cookies, then fill the inside with icing. Gently place icing decorations on and leave the cookies at room temperature until the icing has set, about 2 hours.

2. Use edible ink pens to address the gift tags and enjoy!

Christmassy Rocky Road Fudge,
page 121

CANDY

CANDY CANE SNOWBALLS

These white chocolate snowballs are my favorite holiday treat. This is a classic rocky road recipe that I've altered to taste just like Christmas! Macadamia nuts add a delicious crunch and mini marshmallows give a fluffy surprise in every bite.

4¾ cups high-quality white chocolate
1 cup unsalted butter
½ cup clear corn syrup
1 teaspoon vanilla extract
3 teaspoons peppermint extract
1 cup macadamia nuts
12 candy canes, crushed
½ cup red M&M's
10 ounces mini marshmallows
White and gold sprinkles

1. Place the white chocolate, butter, and corn syrup in a pot over medium-low heat. Stir consistently until completely melted. Then add the vanilla and peppermint extracts. Don't worry if the chocolate and butter have separated.

2. Remove the pot from the heat and allow the mixture to come to room temperature. Stir the mixture with a spatula until the chocolate and butter have fully combined.

3. Add the macadamia nuts, crushed candy canes, red M&M's, and marshmallows and mix until just combined.

4. Divide the mixture between 3 mini muffin containers, and decorate with white and gold sprinkles.

5. Place the snowballs into the fridge until fully set, about 1 to 2 hours. Enjoy!

LUMPS OF COAL

MAKES ABOUT 1 DOZEN

Know anyone who's been naughty this year? This is the recipe for them! These crispy balls use charcoal to get that deep, dark gray color. Charcoal is used in medicine to absorb toxins and chemicals in the gut, however it can also sometimes absorb medication. Make sure to check with your doctor before using charcoal in your recipes. If you are hesitant to use charcoal, black food coloring is a great substitute!

¼ cup butter

5 cups mini marshmallows

½ teaspoon vanilla extract

1 teaspoon food-grade activated charcoal powder

5 cups crispy rice cereal

Cooking spray

1 cup crushed Oreo cookies

1. Melt the butter in a pot over low heat. Add the mini marshmallows and mix until fully melted. Remove from the heat and add the vanilla extract and activated charcoal powder. Add the crispy cereal and mix well.

2. Allow the mixture to cool until it is easily handled. Spray your hands with cooking spray and shape it into balls.

3. Roll the balls in the crushed Oreos, then set aside and cool completely.

SUGARPLUM TRUFFLES

MAKES 2 DOZEN TRUFFLES

These truffles are made with ruby chocolate, which is a type of chocolate that is naturally pink! It has a very delicate berry flavor, so I thought it would be perfect to make these Sugarplum Truffles! I was able to find some ruby chocolate online, but if you're unable to get your hands on it, white chocolate is a great substitute.

½ cup whipping cream
2 cups ruby chocolate, finely chopped
24 small pieces of black licorice
2 cups purple sanding sugar

1. Heat the whipping cream in the microwave for about 1 minute, until hot.

2. Pour the whipping cream on top of the ruby chocolate and let it rest for 2 to 3 minutes. Then stir and mix well until the chocolate has fully melted and combined with the cream.

3. Place the ganache into the fridge and allow to set, about 2 to 3 hours, or overnight.

4. Use a melon baller to scoop little balls of ganache. Roll them in your hands to create a plum shape.

5. Stick a small piece of licorice into the truffle, then roll it in purple sanding sugar. Repeat with the remaining ganache.

6. Enjoy your sweet little plums!

Peppermint Present Truffles

MAKES ABOUT 10 TRUFFLES

These sweet truffles can be served as it, or used as decoration for any festive dessert! This recipe uses pure chocolate (not candy melts), which requires oil-based food coloring when dyeing. Regular food coloring, both liquid and gel, contains water, which causes chocolate to seize. If you are struggling to find oil-based food coloring, you can simply use red and white candy melts instead.

2 cups white chocolate, melted
Red oil-based food coloring
½ cup whipping cream, hot
1 cup white chocolate, finely chopped
1 teaspoon peppermint extract
5 candy canes, finely crushed

1. Divide the melted white chocolate into 2 bowls. Use 2 to 3 drops of food coloring to dye one bowl red. Spoon the chocolate into a square truffle mold to create the chocolate shells, making half of the squares white and half red. Place the mold into the freezer for the chocolate to harden, about 10 to 20 minutes.

2. Pour the hot cream on top of the finely chopped white chocolate and mix well. Add the peppermint extract and candy canes and combine. Chill the ganache in the fridge until thickened, like the consistency of peanut butter. Place the ganache in a piping bag fitted with a #2A (large round) piping tip.

3. Pipe the ganache into the truffle shells. Pour more melted chocolate on top and smooth the surface. Return the chocolates to the freezer for the chocolate to fully harden, about 30 minutes.

4. Unmold the chocolates. Using a toothpick or a piping bag fitted with a #3 (small round) piping tip, draw ribbons and bows onto the chocolates with the remaining red and white chocolate. Draw red bows onto the white boxes and white bows onto the red boxes. Return the truffles to the freezer for a final 10 minutes to set and enjoy!

CHAMPAGNE TEDDY BEAR TRUFFLES

MAKES 18 CHOCOLATES

Champagne and white chocolate are a match made in heaven. These little bears sparkle under the light and are filled with a delicious, creamy champagne ganache filling. For an alcohol-free version, substitute the champagne for sparkling apple juice!

2 cups white chocolate, melted
¼ cup whipping cream
1¼ cups white chocolate, finely chopped
Pinch of salt
3 tablespoons champagne (or sparkling apple juice)
Gold luster dust (optional)

1. Spread some melted white chocolate onto the inside of a silicone bear-shaped mold. Place the mold in the freezer for the chocolate to harden, about 15 minutes. Make sure the sides are completely covered in chocolate, to prevent the filling from leaking out.

2. To make the filling, heat the whipping cream in the microwave for about 30 seconds, until hot. Pour this on top of the finely chopped white chocolate and stir until the chocolate has melted. Add the salt and champagne and mix well. Place the bowl in the freezer for 30 minutes, until the filling has thickened.

3. Pour the filling into the chocolate shells and return the chocolates to the freezer for an additional 30 minutes, for the filling to set as much as possible.

4. Pour the remaining melted white chocolate on top, making sure to fully enclose the filling in the chocolate. The filling is quite runny, so any gaps will allow the filling to leak out. Return to the freezer for a final 20 minutes for the chocolate to fully harden.

5. Remove the chocolates from the mold and if desired, dust with some gold luster dust to give a festive, champagne-like look to them. To store, keep the chocolates in the freezer until ready to serve.

CHRISTMASSY ROCKY ROAD FUDGE

MAKES 2 (9X9-INCH) PANS

This recipe is one of my first that went viral on Instagram—everyone thought I was pouring Christmas candies into macaroni and cheese! In reality, this is a sweet, chocolaty, peppermint slice of goodness. I have been known to eat an entire batch myself, so exercise caution when nibbling. It can be addictive!

4¾ cups good-quality white chocolate
1 cup unsalted butter
½ cup corn syrup
3 teaspoons pure peppermint extract
½ cup macadamia nuts
1¼ cups Christmas-colored candies
   (+ extra for topping)
5 cups mini marshmallows
Candy cane and gingerbread man
   icing decorations

1. Place the white chocolate, butter, and corn syrup in a pot over medium-low heat. Stir consistently until completely melted. Don't worry if the chocolate and butter have separated.

2. Remove from the heat, and stir the mixture with a spatula or a whisk until the chocolate and butter have fully combined. Add the peppermint extract and allow it to slightly cool. Add the macadamia nuts, Christmas candies, and marshmallows, and mix until just combined. Pour the mixture into a square aluminum container, and sprinkle some extra candies and cute icing decorations (mine look like candy canes and gingerbread men) on top. Cover with aluminum foil and place this in the freezer until set, about 1 to 2 hours.

3. Slice the rocky road into bite-sized squares, and you're done! Note: Beware, you will eat this so quickly without realizing it—it's probably the most addictive dessert I've ever made!

CRANBERRY GUMMY BEARS

MAKES ABOUT 3 DOZEN

Cranberries typically only feature in cranberry sauce during the holidays, but they deserve to shine in all their glory! These tart berries are being turned into glistening gummy bears. Serve them in a festive dish or drop a couple into some champagne or sparkling apple juice. The carbonation will make them dance up and down inside the glass!

¼ cup + 2 tablespoons powdered gelatin
⅓ cup water
2 cups cranberry juice
Red food coloring (optional)

1. Sprinkle the gelatin into the water and let develop for 5 minutes.

2. Pour the cranberry juice into a small pot and bring to a simmer. Add the gelatin mixture and whisk until fully dissolved. If desired, add a few drops of red food coloring.

3. Pour the liquid into a container with an easy-pour spout and pour into a gummy bear mold. Place the mold in the fridge until the gummy bears have fully set, about 30 minutes.

4. Eat as is, or pop a couple into champagne glasses and top with champagne for a cute, festive touch to your cocktail!

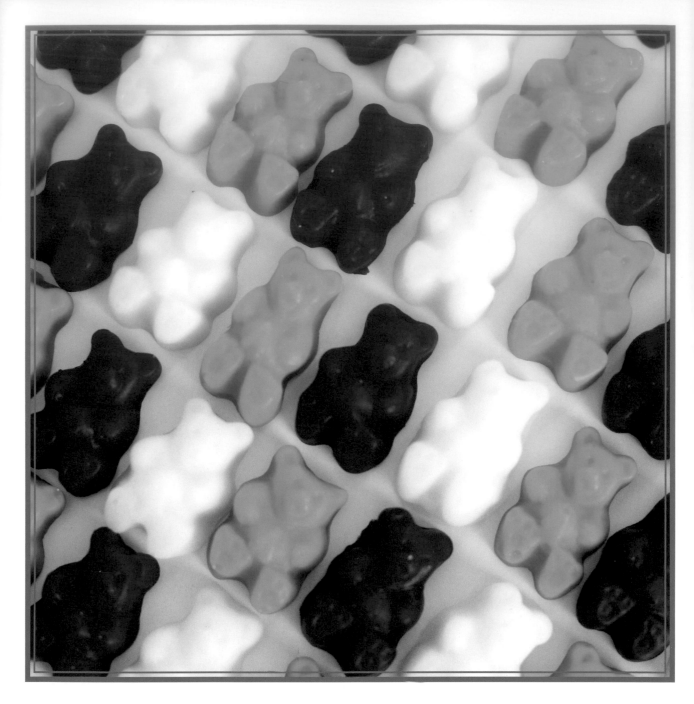

Peppermint Gummy Bears

MAKES ABOUT 3 DOZEN

Gummy bears are my favorite food (seriously), so holiday-flavored bears are a must! These gummy bears taste like sweet peppermint ice cream, thanks to some condensed milk.

1 cup cold water
½ cup powdered gelatin
1 cup sweetened condensed milk
¼ cup sugar
2–3 teaspoons peppermint extract
Red and green food coloring

1. Pour the water and gelatin into a pot and let sit for 10 minutes, until the gelatin has developed.

2. Set the pot to medium-high heat and whisk until the gelatin has dissolved. Add the condensed milk, sugar, and peppermint extract and whisk until fully combined.

3. Divide the mixture into 3 bowls and use 1 to 2 drops of each food coloring to dye one bowl red, one bowl green, and leave the remaining bowl white.

4. Pour the mixture into a gummy bear mold, then transfer to the fridge and allow the gummy bears to set, about 1 hour.

5. Unmold the gummy bears and enjoy! To store, place the gummy bears in an airtight container and store in the fridge.

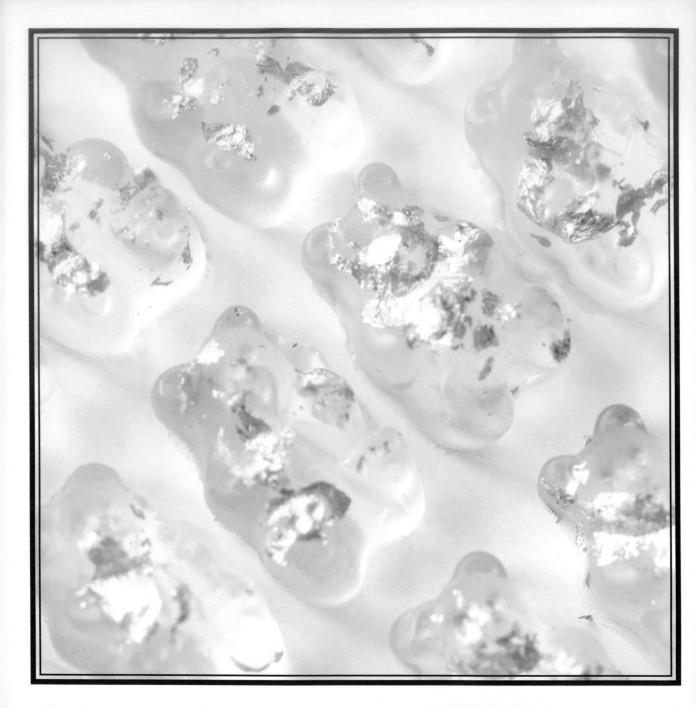

CHAMPAGNE GUMMY BEARS

MAKES ABOUT 3 DOZEN

It's always fun to add a touch of glamor to the holidays! These gummy bears have real gold leaf in them and are made with champagne. For an alcohol-free option, try using sparkling apple juice!

3 tablespoons powdered gelatin
¼ cup water
1 cup champagne (or sparkling apple juice)
Edible gold leaf flakes

1. Sprinkle the gelatin into the water and let develop for 5 minutes.

2. Pour the champagne (or sparkling apple juice) into a small pot and bring to a simmer. Add the gelatin mixture and whisk until fully dissolved. Pour the liquid into a container with an easy-pour spout and cool to room temperature.

3. Sprinkle some gold leaf flakes into the inside of a gummy bear mold and gently pour the liquid on top. Place the mold in the fridge until the gummy bears have fully set, about 30 minutes.

4. Eat as is, package into cellophane bags for a holiday gift, or pop a couple into champagne glasses and top with champagne for a cute, sparkly touch to your cocktail!

GIANT CANDY CANE GUMMY BEAR

MAKES 1 GIANT GUMMY BEAR

Gummy bears are so much fun, but they are even better when they're giant! This gummy bear would be a fantastic surprise stocking stuffer. Change up the color and flavor depending on the recipient and wrap it in a pretty cellophane bag.

2 cups cold water
1 cup powdered gelatin
2 cups (about 2 cans) sweetened condensed
    milk
½ cup sugar
1–2 tablespoons peppermint extract
Red food coloring

1. Pour the water and gelatin into a pot and let sit for 10 minutes, until the gelatin has developed.

2. Set the pot to medium-high heat and whisk until the gelatin has dissolved. Add the condensed milk, sugar, and peppermint extract and whisk until fully combined.

3. Divide the mixture into 2 bowls. Use a couple drops of food coloring to dye one bowl red and leave the remaining bowl white. Chill the mixture in the fridge for 10 to 15 minutes, until it is gloopy and lumpy, but still able to be poured. This will prevent the two colors from mixing together when being poured.

4. Alternating colors, pour the mixture into a giant gummy bear mold then transfer to the fridge and allow the gummy bear to set, about 3 hours.

5. Unmold the gummy bear and enjoy! To store, place the gummy bear in an airtight container and store in the fridge.

Hot Chocolate Fudge

FILLS A 9X9-INCH TRAY

The marshmallows used in this fudge are extra mini! I was able to snag some online and they add a wonderful texture to the smooth and creamy white and dark chocolate fudge.

White Layer:
3¼ cups white chocolate chips
2 tablespoons unsalted butter
1 (10-ounce) can condensed milk
1 teaspoon vanilla extract
Cooking spray

Chocolate Layer:
3¼ cups dark chocolate chips
2 tablespoons unsalted butter
1 (10-ounce) can condensed milk
1 cup mini marshmallow bits

Make the White Layer:

1. Place the white chocolate chips and butter in a microwave-safe bowl and microwave for 1 minute, or until melted. Mix well. Add the condensed milk and vanilla extract and mix to combine.

2. Line a 9x9-inch square pan with foil and spray with cooking spray. Pour the white fudge into the pan and smooth the surface. Set aside.

Make the Chocolate Layer:

1. Place the dark chocolate chips and butter in a microwave-safe bowl and microwave for 1 minute, or until melted. Mix well. Add the condensed milk and mix to combine.

2. Pour on top of the white chocolate layer. Sprinkle some marshmallow bits on top and gently press into the fudge.

3. Chill in the fridge for 2 hours, then slice into squares and enjoy!

Red, Green, and White Christmas Jellies

MAKES ABOUT 15 JELLIES

This is a great recipe to make in advance. When you're ready to serve, just slice and plate!

Red Layer:
1 (3-ounce) box red Jell-O
1½ teaspoons powdered gelatin
1 cup boiling water

Green Layer:
1 (3-ounce) box green Jell-O
1½ teaspoons powdered gelatin
1 cup boiling water

White Layer:
1 (10-ounce) can condensed milk
1½ cups boiling water, divided
½ cup cold water
2 tablespoons powdered gelatin

**Whipped cream and festive sprinkles for
decoration (optional)**

1. Make the red and green layers: Make one color at a time by pouring the contents of one box of Jell-O and 1½ teaspoons of gelatin into a bowl and combine. Add 1 cup of boiling water and mix until everything is completely dissolved. Repeat with the other color in a separate bowl. Set both bowls aside.

2. Make the white layer: Combine the condensed milk and 1 cup boiling water. Pour ½ cup cold water into a bowl and sprinkle powdered gelatin over. Allow this to sit for 2 to 3 minutes, then add ½ cup boiling water and mix well. Add this to the condensed milk mixture and fully combine.

3. Pour ½ cup of the green Jell-O into an 8x5-inch dish lined with plastic wrap. Place in the fridge for 20 minutes, or until fully set. Pour ½ cup of the white layer on top and return to the fridge for 20 minutes. Pour ½ cup of the red Jell-O on top and return to the fridge. Repeat, alternating with red and green layers, making sure to have a white layer in between each color.

4. Once the jelly has fully set, unmold and slice into cubes or use a festive cookie cutter.

5. If desired, top with some whipped cream and festive sprinkles and enjoy!

CRISPY CHRISTMAS TREES

Homemade rice cereal treats are in a league of their own. They are like a cloud of sweet marshmallows—I highly encourage you to try these out! If you'd rather not use a stovetop, step 1 can be done in a microwave-safe bowl.

¼ cup unsalted butter

5 cups mini marshmallows

½ teaspoon vanilla extract

Green food coloring

6 cups crispy rice cereal

Cooking spray

Colorful sprinkles

Confectioners' sugar

1. Melt the butter in a pot over low heat. Add the mini marshmallows and mix until fully melted. Remove from the heat and add the vanilla extract and 3 drops green food coloring. Add the rice cereal and mix well.

2. Allow the mixture to cool until it is easily handled. Spray your hands with cooking spray and shape it into Christmas trees.

3. Roll the trees in colorful sprinkles, then set aside and cool completely.

4. Dust with confectioners' sugar and enjoy!

Snowflake Marshmallows

This is one of my favorite recipes I've made! These beautiful, delicate marshmallows sit on top of your hot chocolate and look like it's snowing in your mug!

⅓ cup + ¼ cup cold water, separated
2½ teaspoons powdered gelatin
1 cup sugar
½ teaspoon vanilla extract, or seeds
   from ½ vanilla bean pod
Cornstarch

1. Draw circles onto a sheet of parchment paper using the rim of your desired mug. This will ensure that the marshmallows will fit into your cup. Draw snowflakes inside the circles. Flip the sheet of parchment paper over and place on a baking sheet.

2. Pour ⅓ cup of cold water into the bowl of an electric mixer and sprinkle the powdered gelatin on top. Let sit for 5 minutes.

3. Place the sugar and ¼ cup cold water in a small pot and set to medium-high heat. Stir until the sugar has melted.

4. Attach a candy thermometer to the pot and boil the sugar until it reaches 238°F. Brush the sides of the pot with a wet pastry brush if sugar crystals stick to the sides.

5. Add the hot sugar to the gelatin and stir the mixture by hand whisking for a few minutes to slightly cool. Then beat with an electric mixer on medium-high speed for 8 to 10 minutes, until soft peaks form. Then add the vanilla and mix well.

6. Place the marshmallow mixture in a piping bag fitted with a narrow round tip. Pipe the marshmallows following the lines on the parchment paper. Work quickly, as the marshmallow stiffens quickly. Let the marshmallows stiffen for 1 hour.

7. Dust the marshmallows with cornstarch and gently peel them off the parchment paper. Flip them over and dust the undersides with cornstarch. Bounce them in a sieve to remove any excess and enjoy! To store, place them in a single layer in a zip-top bag.

CANDY CANE MARSHMALLOWS

These marshmallows not only look like candy canes, they taste like them, too! Spoil yourself this winter and hook one onto your hot chocolate mug.

Cooking spray
⅓ cup + ¼ cup cold water, separated
2½ teaspoons powdered gelatin
1 cup sugar
1 teaspoon peppermint extract
Hot pink food coloring
¼ cup cornstarch
¼ cup confectioners' sugar

1. Line a 9x9-inch square dish with parchment paper and grease the paper with cooking spray.

2. Pour ⅓ cup of cold water into the bowl of an electric mixer and sprinkle the powdered gelatin on top. Let sit for 5 minutes.

3. Place the sugar and ¼ cup cold water in a small pot and set to medium-high heat. Stir until the sugar has melted.

4. Attach a candy thermometer to the pot and boil the sugar until it reaches 238°F. Brush the sides of the pot with a wet pastry brush if sugar crystals stick to the sides. Add the peppermint extract and mix well.

5. Add the hot sugar to the gelatin and stir the mixture by hand, whisking for a few minutes to slightly cool. Then beat with an electric mixer on medium-high speed for 8 to 10 minutes, until soft peaks form.

6. Pour the marshmallow into the dish and dot with the hot pink food coloring. Use a toothpick to swirl the color around to create a pretty pattern. Allow the marshmallow to set for 3 to 4 hours (or up to overnight) until firm.

7. Combine the cornstarch and confectioners' sugar in a bowl. Dip a candy cane–shaped cookie cutter into the cornstarch mixture and cut out candy canes from the marshmallow. Flip the candy canes over and use a sieve to dust the underside with the cornstarch mixture. Place the marshmallows in an empty sieve and bounce a few times to remove any excess powder.

REINDEER MARSHMALLOWS

MAKES 12-15 MARSHMALLOWS

If you've tasted homemade marshmallows before, you know there is nothing better! These vanilla marshmallows look like sweet little reindeer, and make the perfect treat to enjoy at home or for gifting in tiny favor bags.

⅓ cup + ¼ cup cold water, separated
2½ teaspoons powdered gelatin
1 cup sugar
¼ cup cold water
1 teaspoon vanilla extract, or seeds from
  1 vanilla bean
26–30 mini candy canes
12–15 red candy melts
26–30 chocolate chips

1. Pour ⅓ cup of cold water into the bowl of an electric mixer and sprinkle the powdered gelatin on top. Let sit for 5 minutes.

2. Place the sugar and ¼ cup cold water in a small pot and set to medium-high heat. Stir until the sugar has melted.

3. Attach a candy thermometer to the pot and boil the sugar until it reaches 238°F. Brush the sides of the pot with a wet pastry brush if sugar crystals stick to the sides.

4. Add the hot sugar to the gelatin and stir the mixture by hand, whisking for a few minutes to slightly cool. Then beat with an electric mixer on medium-high speed for 8 to 10 minutes, until soft peaks form. Then add the vanilla and mix well.

5. Place the marshmallow mixture in a piping bag fitted with a #2A (large, round) piping tip. Place sets of 2 candy canes side by side onto a baking sheet lined with parchment paper or a Silpat mat. Pipe the marshmallows into a very large circle, then add 2 dollops on top for the ears. Work quickly, as the marshmallow stiffens quickly.

6. Stick a red candy melt into the center as the nose and 2 chocolate chips as the eyes. Let the marshmallows stiffen at room temperature overnight.

7. Gently use a butter knife to remove the marshmallows from the pan. Enjoy!

GINGERBREAD MAN MARSHMALLOWS

MAKES 10 LARGE MARSHMALLOWS

These little gingerbread men are as light as air and packed with flavor!

⅓ cup + ¼ cup cold water, divided
2½ teaspoons powdered gelatin
1 cup sugar
Gingerbread Spice Mix (page 147)
Brown food coloring
¼ cup cornstarch
¼ cup confectioners' sugar

1. Line a 9x9-inch square pan with parchment paper and grease the paper with some oil.

2. Pour ⅓ cup of cold water into the bowl of an electric mixer and sprinkle the powdered gelatin on top. Let sit for 5 minutes.

3. Place the sugar and ¼ cup cold water in a small pot and set to medium-high heat. Stir until the sugar has melted.

4. Attach a candy thermometer to the pot and boil the sugar until it reaches 238°F. Brush the sides of the pot with a wet pastry brush if sugar crystals stick to the sides.

5. Add the hot sugar to the gelatin and stir the mixture by hand whisking for a few minutes to slightly cool. Then beat with an electric mixer on medium-high speed for 8 to 10 minutes, until soft peaks form. Then add the Gingerbread Spice Mix and 2 to 3 drops brown food coloring and mix well.

6. Pour the marshmallow mixture into the pan and let it set at room temperature for 2 to 3 hours (or up to overnight), until the marshmallow is firm.

7. Combine the cornstarch and confectioners' sugar in a bowl. Dust the surface of the marshmallows in the cornstarch mixture. Dip a gingerbread man cookie cutter into the cornstarch mixture and cut out gingerbread man shapes. Flip the marshmallows over and coat the underside in a layer of the cornstarch mixture. Bounce the marshmallows in a sieve to remove any excess powder and enjoy!

Christmas Pudding Cream Puffs, page 163

Other Treats & Extras

GINGERBREAD SPICE MIX

MAKES ABOUT ¼ CUP

This is such a delicious gingerbread mix! It's used in numerous recipes throughout this book and can be stored in a jar for easy access during your holiday baking.

1 tablespoon + 1 teaspoon ground
   cinnamon
1 tablespoon ground allspice
1 tablespoon ground ginger
1½ teaspoons ground nutmeg
1½ teaspoons ground cloves

1. Combine all spices in a bowl.

2. Place them into a mason jar or sealed container to use for a variety of these recipes!

Strawberry Cheesecake Santas

MAKES ABOUT 12 SANTAS

This is one of the first recipes I ever made on YouTube, and I still love it to this day! The fresh, vibrant strawberries pair wonderfully with the cream cheese filling. And look at those little faces—who could resist?

4 tablespoons butter, room temperature
5 ounces cream cheese, room temperature
¾ cup confectioners' sugar
½ teaspoon vanilla extract
12 strawberries
Festive toothpicks
24 small chocolate chips

1. Cream the butter and cream cheese in a mixing bowl with an electric mixer. Mix in the confectioners' sugar and vanilla with a rubber spatula. Place in the freezer for approximately 20 minutes to allow the filling to stiffen.

2. Wash and thoroughly dry the strawberries with a paper towel. Slice off the tip and leafy base of each strawberry, then slice the strawberry in half width-wise. Dry the sliced surfaces with a paper towel.

3. Place the cream cheese frosting into a piping bag fitted with a #10 (medium round) piping tip. Position the strawberry so that it is pointing upward and sitting flat on your work surface. Pipe a generous dollop of frosting between the layers of the strawberry. Place the top layer of strawberry on top and gently insert a toothpick down into the strawberry, to secure the layers together.

4. Place a small dollop of frosting at the tip of the strawberry, to look like the fluff on Santa's hat.

5. Stick small chocolate chips onto the cream cheese filling as the eyes.

6. Refrigerate the Santas until they are ready to be served.

TIP: If you would like to make these Santas even more cheesecake-like, sprinkle some graham cracker crumbs onto your serving dish before adding them.

Evergreen Christmas Tree Matcha Blondies

MAKES 8 BLONDIES

These delicious blondies are baked in a pre-segmented pan. If you don't have one available, simply use an 8-inch round cake pan!

Blondie Batter:
Cooking spray
1 cup unsalted butter, melted
2 cups light brown sugar
2 large eggs
2 teaspoons vanilla extract
1 teaspoon almond extract
½ teaspoon salt
2 cups all-purpose flour
3 tablespoons matcha green
    tea powder

Buttercream (page 11)
2 tablespoons matcha green
    tea powder

Bake the Blondies:

1. Grease a triangular cake pan with cooking spray (or use an 8-inch round cake pan). Preheat the oven to 350°F.

2. Pour the melted butter and brown sugar into a mixing bowl and beat with an electric mixer until combined. Add the eggs, extracts, and salt and mix well. Add the flour and matcha and mix until well combined.

3. Fill your prepared pan with the batter and bake for 20 to 25 minutes, until the edges are just starting to brown. Cool completely.

To Decorate:

1. Set aside about ¼ of the buttercream and add the matcha to the larger amount. Mix well.

2. Use a variety of piping tips to pipe different styles of trees onto the blondies. For the green and white effect, simply spread both colors of buttercream into the piping bag, then pipe away!

Tree 1: #2A (large round) piping tip. Start at the top of the tree and pipe a continuous wave of buttercream all the way down to the base of the tree.

Tree 2: #2D (large star/flower) piping tip. Hold the piping bag perpendicular to the tree and pipe dollops of buttercream all over.

Tree 3: #2A (large round) piping tip. Start at the base of the tree. Pipe a row of dollops. Use a butter knife to drag the dollops upward. Repeat to the top of the tree.

Tree 4: #19 (small star) piping tip. Hold the piping bag perpendicular to the tree and pipe dollops of buttercream all over.

(Continued on next page)

Tree 5: #104 (medium petal) piping tip. Position the tree so that the tip is facing you. Hold the piping bag so that it is parallel to the tree, with the widest part of the piping tip closest to the tree. Starting at the base of the tree, pipe vertical waves of buttercream toward the tip of the tree. Repeat until the tree is covered.

Tree 6: #104 (medium petal) piping tip. Spread white buttercream onto the side of the piping bag in line with the wide end of the piping tip. Fill in the rest of the space with green buttercream. To decorate, start at the base of the tree and position the piping bag so that the white buttercream is at the bottom of each "branch." Pipe a row of buttercream in a scallop pattern. Repeat until you reach the tip of the tree.

Tree 7: #69 (medium leaf) piping tip. Starting at the base of the tree, pipe little branches of buttercream, pulling the piping bag toward the base of the tree as you pipe. Repeat until you reach the tip of the tree.

Tree 8: #2D (large star/flower) piping tip. When filling the piping bag, swirl the white and green buttercream together. To decorate, start at the base of the tree. Pipe a row of dollops. Use a palette knife or butter knife to drag the dollops upward. Repeat to the top of the tree.

Candy Cane Ganache Tarts

These tarts have a sugar cookie crust and are filled with the smoothest, creamiest white chocolate peppermint ganache. This ganache is amazing because we are whipping it, which gives it a very light and creamy texture. Once you taste whipped ganache, you'll never go back to regular ganache again!

Tart Shells:
1 cup all-purpose flour
Pinch of salt
¼ teaspoon baking powder
¼ cup unsalted butter, room temperature
½ cup sugar
1 tablespoon milk
½ egg, beaten
½ teaspoon vanilla extract
Red food coloring
Cooking spray
½ cup white chocolate, melted
1 cup crushed candy canes

Ganache Filling:
1½ cups good-quality white chocolate, melted
½ cup whipping cream, heated until hot
½ teaspoon vanilla extract
1 teaspoon peppermint extract
Pinch of salt
Red food coloring

Make the Tart Shells:

1. Mix together the flour, salt, and baking powder in a bowl. In a separate bowl, cream the butter and sugar with an electric mixer until it becomes light and fluffy. Add the milk, egg, and vanilla extract and mix well. Slowly add the flour mixture until it is just combined.

2. Shape the dough into a ball, then divide it into 2. Dye one ball red with a few drops of the red food coloring.

3. Gently swirl both colors of dough together in your hands a couple times, then roll the dough out onto a floured surface. Cut out circles with a 4½-inch round cookie cutter.

4. Spray a regular-sized muffin pan with cooking spray and press the rounds into the bottom and sides of the tin. Place the muffin tin in the freezer for 15 minutes for the dough to stiffen.

5. Bake at 350°F for 10 minutes, until the edges are golden. Allow the tarts to fully cool in the pan, then gently remove them from the tin with the tip of a butter knife.

(Continued on page 155)

6. Dip the edges of the tarts into white chocolate, then roll in the crushed candy canes. Place the tart shells in the fridge for the white chocolate to set.

Make the Ganache Filling:
1. Combine the melted white chocolate, hot whipping cream, vanilla extract, peppermint extract, and salt in a bowl. Divide the mixture in half and dye one bowl red with a couple drops of food coloring.

2. Place the bowls into the fridge until the ganache has stiffened, 1 to 2 hours.

3. Beat each individual ganache with an electric mixer until stiff peaks form. Spread each color of ganache vertically into a piping bag fitted with a #1A (large, round) piping tip, so that each color creates a vertical stripe inside the bag.

Assembly:
1. Pipe the ganache into the tarts in a swirling motion.

Dancing Reindeer Brioche

MAKES ABOUT A 13X7-INCH REINDEER

This delicious homemade brioche is filled with chocolate! Slice it up for breakfast and put a smile on everyone's face. This recipe is quite sentimental to me, as I first created it at the beginning of my YouTube career. I wasn't making any money at the time, and, as I was making the brioche, I was stressed about how my future would look. Now as I sit here, adding this recipe to my third cookbook, I feel so much gratitude to all of you. Thank you for making my dreams come true.

1 batch Brioche Dough (page 15)
4 ounces dark chocolate, roughly chopped
2 raisins
1 egg, beaten
3 tablespoons red-colored chocolate, melted

1. Line a baking sheet with parchment paper and preheat the oven to 350°F.

2. Roll ⅔ of the Brioche Dough into a long rectangle. Sprinkle ¾ of the dark chocolate into the center and roll it into a log. Shape it into the reindeer's body and place it on a baking sheet lined with parchment paper.

3. Take about ⅔ of the remaining brioche and roll it out into a circle shape. Place the remaining dark chocolate in the center and seal the dough closed to create a bun. Shape it into the reindeer's head and attach it to the body. Use the remaining dough to make the feet, nose, and antlers. To make the antlers, make 2 little logs of dough and trim the edges with scissors to create a scalloped pattern. Attach these to the reindeer. Stick the raisins onto the reindeer to make its eyes. Brush the entire surface with a beaten egg.

4. Bake for 35 to 40 minutes until golden brown. Remove from the oven and let slightly cool. Spread the red-colored chocolate onto the nose and enjoy!

CHRISTMAS LIGHT OREO BITES

MAKES 9-10 TRUFFLES

These truffles taste like Oreo cheesecake—they are fabulous. We're rolling them in colored sugar to make them sparkle just like real Christmas tree lights!

2 cups Oreo cookie crumbs
9 ounces cream cheese, room temperature
9–10 mini chocolate peanut butter cups
Silver edible metallic spray
2 cups each pink, blue, and yellow candy melts, melted
1 cup each pink, blue, and yellow sanding sugar

1. Place the cookie crumbs and cream cheese in a bowl and beat with an electric mixer until fully combined.

2. Divide the mixture into 9–10 pieces and shape into Christmas light shapes. Place them on a plate lined with plastic wrap and refrigerate until firm, about 1 hour.

3. Place the peanut butter cups on a sheet of parchment paper, with the largest side facing down. Spray all over with silver edible metallic spray. Set aside.

4. To add the coating to the truffles, place a truffle on a fork and submerge it in one color of the melted candy melts. Allow the excess candy melts to drip off, then roll in the coordinating sugar. It may take a few minutes for the candy melts to set, so keep the truffle in the bowl of sprinkles until the candy melt coating feels stiff. Repeat with the remaining truffles.

5. Dip the base of the peanut butter cups into some extra melted candy melts and stick one on each truffle.

Reindeer Chocolate Hazelnut Cheesecake Pops

MAKES 12 POPS

Decorated cake "popsicles" are a fun trend, especially when they're made with cheesecake. This cheesecake recipe is so creamy, you'll be reaching for more!

14 ounces cream cheese, room temperature
¼ cup + 2 tablespoons granulated sugar
1¾ cups whipping cream
¼ cup lemon juice
½ teaspoon vanilla extract
½ cup chocolate hazelnut spread
2½ teaspoons powdered gelatin
3 tablespoons water
2 cups chocolate candy melts, melted
12 popsicle sticks
12 red candy melts (not melted)
12 pretzels, broken in half
Edible gold spray
Black food coloring

Make the Cheesecake Filling:

1. Place the cream cheese and sugar in a bowl and beat with an electric mixer until smooth. Add the whipping cream, lemon juice, vanilla extract, and chocolate hazelnut spread, and mix well.

2. In a separate, microwave-safe bowl, combine the gelatin and water. Microwave for 30 seconds, or until melted. Add this to the cheesecake mixture and beat to combine. Set aside.

Assembly:

1. Line the inside of a flat cakesicle mold with the melted chocolate. This mold should be a flat mold, not a traditional vertical popsicle mold. If your mold has a space to insert popsicle sticks, insert them now. Otherwise, insert them in step 3.

2. Place the mold into the fridge for 10 to 15 minutes, until the candy melts have set.

3. Fill the mold with the cheesecake filling, then seal closed with more candy melts. Return the mold to the fridge for 1 to 2 hours, until both the cheesecake and candy melts have set.

4. Gently unmold the pops and place them on a plate. Use some extra chocolate candy melts to attach a red candy melt nose to each pop. Return to the fridge.

5. Place the pretzels on a sheet of parchment paper. Spray with some edible gold spray and allow to dry for 10 to15 minutes. Use some extra chocolate candy melts to attach the antlers to the pops.

6. Dip a small, food-safe paintbrush into some black food coloring and paint the eyes onto the pops. Enjoy!

CHRISTMAS PUDDING CREAM PUFFS

MAKES ABOUT 15 CREAM PUFFS

A fun twist on a Christmas classic! These delicious cream puffs are filled with homemade chocolate pastry cream and decorated to look like Christmas pudding.

Cream Puffs:

1 cup water
½ cup unsalted butter, cold and cut into cubes
1 teaspoon sugar
½ teaspoon salt
1 cup all-purpose flour
¼ cup cocoa powder
4 large eggs

Pastry Cream:

½ cup sugar
¼ cup cornstarch
Pinch of salt
2 cups milk
4 large egg yolks
1 tablespoon cocoa powder
1½ teaspoons vanilla extract
2 tablespoons unsalted butter, cold

Glaze:

1 cup confectioners' sugar
3 tablespoons whipping cream
Red and green piping gel

Make the Cream Puffs:

1. Line a baking sheet with parchment paper and preheat the oven to 375°F.

2. In a large pot, combine the water, butter, sugar, and salt. Set to high heat and bring to a boil. Stir in the flour and cocoa powder with a wooden spoon and mix until a film forms on the bottom of the pan (the pan will lose its shine and look more matte). Transfer the dough to a bowl and cool for 3 to 4 minutes. Add the eggs one at a time, stirring vigorously and completely incorporating each egg after each addition.

3. Transfer the dough to a piping bag fitted with a large, round piping tip and pipe 1½-inch rounds onto your prepared baking sheets. Wet your fingers and smooth any pointed peaks.

4. Bake them for 30 minutes. Cool on the pan for 10 minutes, then transfer to a wire rack and cool completely.

Make the Pastry Cream:

1. Combine the sugar, cornstarch, and salt in a pot. Add the milk, egg yolks, and cocoa powder and whisk together. Set to medium heat and whisk constantly until the mixture comes to a boil. Once it thickens, remove from the heat and add the vanilla extract and butter.

2. Strain through a sieve and cover with plastic wrap, pressing it directly on the surface. Refrigerate until chilled. If the pastry cream becomes lumpy, pulse in a food processor a couple times. Transfer to a piping bag fitted with a round tip.

3. Poke holes in the base of the cream puffs and fill with pastry cream.

To Decorate:

1. Combine the confectioners' sugar and whipping cream in a bowl. Spoon over the cream puffs.

2. Pipe holly onto the top of each cream puff with the piping gel. Enjoy!

Christmas Pudding Oreos

MAKES 10

These are a sweet, easy treat! Perfect for making with young kids and ideal as a festive addition to lunchboxes or to Santa's cookie tray.

10 Oreo cookies
2 cups melted milk chocolate
¼ cup holly sprinkles

1. Place one cookie on a fork and submerge it into the melted milk chocolate. Allow any excess chocolate to drip off, then place on a baking sheet lined with parchment paper.

2. Place some holly sprinkles on top, then transfer the cookies to the fridge for the chocolate to set, about 30 minutes.

3. Enjoy with a cup of tea or hot chocolate!

Baby Spruce Tree Cheesecake Cups

FILLS 4 (2½-INCH) TERRA-COTTA POTS

These adorable little spruce trees are sitting atop a creamy and smooth chocolate cheesecake base. They are perfect as a light dessert or a fun after-school snack!

Cheesecake Filling:
8 ounces cream cheese, room temperature
¼ cup granulated sugar
2 tablespoons cocoa powder
2 tablespoons Bailey's liqueur (optional)
Mini Oreo cookies
Mini food-safe terra-cotta pots

Baby Spruce Trees:
1 cup Buttercream (page 11)
½ cup marshmallow crème
Green food coloring
2 tablespoons festive sprinkles

Make the Cheesecake Filling:

1. Beat the cream cheese, sugar, and cocoa powder with an electric mixer until smooth. Add the Bailey's liqueur, if using, and mix to combine.

2. Place mini Oreo cookies into the bottom of mini terra-cotta pots. Spoon the cheesecake filling into the pots and chill in the fridge while you make the trees.

Make the Spruce Trees:

1. Beat the vanilla frosting and marshmallow crème with an electric mixer until well combined. Dye the frosting a vibrant green color.

2. Place in a piping bag fitted with a #27 (small star) piping tip.

3. Remove the pots from the fridge and pipe a tall dollop of frosting on top of each pot. Starting at the base and working upward, pipe star shapes and create a pine tree. Decorate with sprinkles.

4. Return the pots to the fridge and chill for 30 minutes.

Candy Cane Doughnuts

MAKES 6 DOUGHNUTS

These doughnuts always put a smile on my face. Not only are they delicious and festive, a subscriber made these for an office baking competition and won! Baked doughnuts are usually quite dense, but these are very delicate and moist.

Doughnut Batter:
1 cup all-purpose flour
1 teaspoon baking powder
¼ teaspoon salt
3 tablespoons unsalted butter, melted
¼ cup sugar
2 tablespoons honey
1 large egg
¼ teaspoon vanilla extract
1 teaspoon peppermint extract
⅓ cup + 1 tablespoon buttermilk
Red food coloring

Glaze:
3 tablespoons whipping cream
½ cup confectioners' sugar
2 cups crushed candy canes

Bake the Doughnuts:

1. Preheat the oven to 400°F. and grease a donut pan.

2. Whisk together the flour, baking powder, and salt in a small bowl and set aside. In a large bowl, combine the butter, sugar, honey, egg, vanilla, and peppermint extract. Add the buttermilk and mix until combined. Add the dry ingredients and mix until just combined, making sure not to over mix. Divide the mixture into 2 bowls and dye one bowl red with a few drops of food coloring.

3. Spoon the batter into a piping bag, placing the piping bag on its side and filling one side with one color, then spoon the other color on top. This will create a striped pattern when you pipe the batter into the pan! Pipe the batter into your prepared doughnut pan and bake for 7 minutes. Cool for 1 minute in the pan, then flip the pan over to remove the doughnuts and cool completely on a wire rack.

Make the Glaze and Decorate:

1. Whisk together the whipping cream and the confectioners' sugar and whisk until fully combined. Dunk each doughnut into the glaze and return to the wire rack. Top with crushed candy canes and enjoy!

REINDEER TART

This tart is sweet, chocolaty, and has a surprise citrus cranberry curd in the middle! I served this to my family and friends after shooting it for this book and received rave reviews for days on end. If you're looking for a holiday dessert that is a guaranteed to be a crowd-pleaser, try this one out!

Crust and Cookies:

1½ cups unsalted butter, room temperature

¾ cup confectioners' sugar

1½ teaspoons vanilla extract

3 cups all-purpose flour

3 tablespoons cocoa powder

1½ teaspoons salt

Cranberry Curd:

3 cups cranberries (fresh or frozen)

¼ cup water

1½ cups brown sugar

5 egg yolks

Zest from 1 orange

¼ cup lemon juice

3 tablespoons cornstarch

¼ cup unsalted butter, cold and cut into cubes

2 teaspoons vanilla extract

Chocolate Ganache Topping:

6 ounces semisweet chocolate, finely chopped

¾ cup whipping cream, microwaved until hot

Cranberry Jellies (page 123, but instead of a gummy bear mold, pour into a flat pan and cut into cubes once firm)

Gold sprinkles

Royal Icing (page 99)

1 fresh orange

Make the Crust and Cookies:

1. Beat the butter with an electric mixer until pale and fluffy. Add the confectioners' sugar and beat for 2 minutes, until well combined. Add the vanilla and combine.

2. In a separate bowl, combine the flour, cocoa powder, and salt. Add the butter mixture and mix until the dough sticks together when pinched. Shape into a ball, wrap in plastic wrap, and chill in the fridge until firm, about 1 hour.

3. Preheat the oven to 325°F. Roll the dough out on a floured surface to ¼ inch thick. Place a 9-inch scalloped tart pan into the center of the dough as a guide and cut a circle of dough 1 inch larger than the pan. Press this circle of dough into the pan. Make sure the dough is pressed into the bottom and the sides.

4. Reroll remaining dough out onto a floured surface and use a reindeer cookie cutter to cut out 3 reindeer. Place the cookies on a baking sheet lined with parchment paper.

5. Bake both the cookies and the tart for 13 to 15 minutes until the edges are lightly browned, keeping the tart in longer than the cookies. Cool both the tart and cookies completely.

6. Once the cookies have cooled, it's time to decorate them! Place the royal icing in a piping bag fitted with a #4 (small round) piping tip. Use the icing to pipe decorative accents, hooves, antlers, and tails onto the deer. Allow the icing to dry completely.

(Continued on next page)

Make the Cranberry Curd:

1. Place the cranberries and water in a pot set to medium. Heat until the berries burst, about 10 to 15 minutes. Place into a blender and pulse until very smooth. Transfer it back into the pot.

2. Add the brown sugar, egg yolks, and orange zest. Stir to combine. In a separate bowl, whisk together the lemon juice and cornstarch. Add this to the curd and stir. Return the pot to medium heat. Cook until the mixture has thickened, making sure to stir constantly.

3. Remove from the heat. Gradually add the butter and whisk to combine. Stir in the vanilla. Allow the curd to cool for 10 minutes, then pour into the tart shell. Place in the fridge for 1 hour, or until the surface of the curd has set.

Make the Ganache:

1. Place the chocolate in a bowl and pour the hot cream on top. Allow it to sit for 3 to 5 minutes, then stir and fully combine the cream and chocolate. Allow the ganache to cool to the touch, then pour it onto the cranberry curd. Smooth the surface with a spatula and chill the tart in the fridge overnight.

To Decorate:

1. Place the reindeer onto the tart. Scatter the cranberry jellies and gold sprinkles around them. Use a vegetable peeler to peel thin strips off the orange. If the peel is too wide, cut them in half. Gently curl the peel with your fingers, then place on the tart. Slice up the tart and enjoy the festive flavors!

CHRISTMAS CROISSANTS

Croissants are my favorite breakfast treat, and I love carrying that over to the holidays. These croissants are so incredibly soft and delicious. This recipe may seem intimidating, but just follow it step by step and you'll have amazing croissants in no time!

Red Dough:
2¼ teaspoons dry active yeast
3 tablespoons warm water
2 tablespoons sugar
1 teaspoon salt
2 tablespoons unsalted butter, melted
1 cup milk
Red food coloring
2½ cups all-purpose flour

Green Dough:
2¼ teaspoons dry active yeast
3 tablespoons warm water
2 tablespoons sugar
1 teaspoon salt
2 tablespoons unsalted butter, melted
1 cup milk
2½ cups all-purpose flour
Green food coloring

2 cups unsalted butter, room temperature

1. First, make the red dough. Place the yeast and warm water in the bowl of a stand mixer. Allow the yeast to develop, for about 5 minutes, until very foamy.

2. Add the sugar, salt, melted butter, milk, and several drops of red food coloring. Attach a dough hook and mix on medium speed until fully combined. Add the flour ½ cup at a time, mixing until the dough becomes sticky and shapes into a ball, about 3 minutes.

3. Transfer the dough to a floured baking sheet and spread out to ½ inch thick. Wrap tightly in plastic wrap and chill in the fridge for 1 hour.

4. Repeat the steps above to make the green dough.

5. Place 1 cup butter onto the center of a sheet of parchment paper and use a spatula to shape the butter into a 6x8-inch rectangle. Place another sheet of parchment paper on top, then transfer everything to a plate and refrigerate until the butter is cold and stiff, about 1 hour. Repeat with the remaining 1 cup butter, to create a total of 2 rectangles of butter.

6. Place the red dough on a floured surface and roll out to a 16x10-inch rectangle, with the short side closest to you. Remove one rectangle of butter from the parchment paper and place in the center of the dough. Take one short end and fold over the entire surface of the butter, pressing the edges together to seal. Repeat with the remaining short end of dough,

(Continued on page 175)

folding over the butter and pressing to seal closed. Roll the dough out into a 16x10-inch rectangle, with a short end facing you. Fold the bottom third of the dough into the center, then fold the top third down. Reshape until the dough measures 11x6 inches. Wrap the dough in plastic wrap and place in the fridge for 45 minutes.

7. Roll the dough out on a floured surface to a 16x10-inch rectangle. Fold the bottom third of the dough into the center, then fold the top third down. Wrap the dough in plastic wrap and return to the fridge to chill for 30 minutes. Repeat this process 2 more times—rolling and folding the dough, chilling it for 45 minutes between each process. Once you have folded the dough the final time, wrap the dough in plastic wrap and chill in the fridge for 4 hours, or up to overnight. Repeat these steps with the green dough and the remaining rectangle of butter.

8. Slice each color of dough in half, creating 2 squares per color. Wrap one red and one green square in plastic wrap and place in the fridge while you use the other two squares of dough. Place the red square of dough onto a floured work surface and roll out into a 9x18-inch rectangle. Repeat with the green dough, then place on top of the red dough, sealing together with the help of the rolling pin. Slice the dough in half lengthwise, then cut into 7 or 8 triangles. Cut a small slice into the base of each triangle. Roll the triangles into croissant shapes, then gently shape into a crescent shape. Repeat with the remaining dough in the fridge.

9. Place the croissants on a baking sheet, spacing them about 3 inches apart. Cover with a clean dish towel, place in a warm spot, and let rise for 1½ hours.

10. Bake at 425°F for 10 minutes, then cover loosely with aluminum foil and bake for an additional 5 minutes, or until golden brown. Place the baking sheet on a wire rack and cool until warm. Enjoy your freshly baked croissants!

CANDY CANE ICE CREAM

FILLS A 2-LITER CONTAINER

This is my favorite no-churn ice cream recipe! We're adding peppermint and crushed candy canes, creating a marbled peppermint dream! This recipe is also egg-free, which is perfect for those with allergies.

2 cups whipping cream
1 (14 ounce) can condensed milk
1 teaspoon vanilla extract
3 teaspoons peppermint extract
Red and green food coloring
⅓ cup crushed candy canes

1. Beat the whipping cream with an electric mixer until stiff peaks forms.

2. In a separate bowl, combine the condensed milk, vanilla extract, and peppermint extract. Add a large dollop of whipped cream and mix until combined. Add the remaining whipped cream and gently fold until combined.

3. Divide the mixture into 3 bowls. Using a couple drops each, dye one bowl green, one bowl red, and leave the remaining bowl white. Divide the crushed candy canes between all 3 bowls and gently fold to combine.

4. Spoon dollops of each color into a plastic Tupperware container. We recommend using a clear Tupperware container, so that you can see the pattern from the outside!

5. Seal the Tupperware container closed, then freeze for 6 hours, or until stiff.

6. Scoop with an ice cream scoop to create little ice cream globes! Enjoy!

Ugly Christmas Sweater Toast

MAKES 1

A wonderful snack for Christmas morning! Provide a variety of toppings and sprinkles in little ramekins and enjoy a festive, playful breakfast with your friends and family.

Food coloring
½ cup cream cheese, room temperature
   (you won't use it all on one piece of
   toast, don't worry!)
1 slice of toast (per person)
Festive sprinkles and candies

1. Using a couple drops of food coloring, dye the cream cheese your desired holiday colors. Blue and white create a wintry feel, while red and green give a more classic, Christmas style.

2. First, spread your base color onto the entire surface of your toast. Place your accent color cream cheese into a piping bag fitted with either a #18 (small star) or #9 (small round) piping tip. Use a skewer to mark the sleeves into the base color. Use the accent color to create the collar, sleeve, and hem accents.

3. Use sprinkles and candies to decorate the sweaters and create fun patterns.

4. Enjoy your fun, festive breakfast!

EGGNOG PANCAKES

MAKES ABOUT 10 MEDIUM PANCAKES

Pancakes are one of my favorite breakfast foods, and these are extra festive, making them perfect for Christmas morning! Both the batter and the glaze contain eggnog, guaranteeing you tons of flavor.

Pancakes:
1 cup all-purpose flour
2 tablespoons sugar
2 teaspoons baking powder
½ teaspoon salt
1 cup eggnog
2 tablespoons unsalted butter, melted
1 large egg
Cooking spray, for frying pan

Glaze:
1 cup confectioners' sugar
2 tablespoons eggnog
1 tablespoon maple syrup
½ teaspoon rum (or rum extract)
Red, green, and white sprinkles

Make the Pancakes:

1. Combine the flour, sugar, baking powder, and salt in a bowl. In a larger bowl, combine the eggnog, butter, and egg, and whisk until fully combined. Add the dry ingredients and whisk together, but make sure not to overmix. Some lumps are fine!

2. Heat a frying pan over medium heat and spray with cooking spray. Dollop 2 to 3 tablespoons of batter onto the frying pan and smooth the surface with the spoon. Cook until the surface of the pancakes develop some bubbles, about 1 to 2 minutes. Flip and cook for an additional 1 to 2 minutes, or until the surface has browned. Continue with the rest of the batter.

Make the Glaze:

1. Combine the confectioners' sugar, eggnog, maple syrup, and rum in a small bowl. Drizzle over the pancakes and top with festive sprinkles. Enjoy!

Gingerbread House Mug Toppers

MAKES ABOUT 6-8 HOUSES

These sweet little houses rest atop the rim of your mug and add an adorable, festive touch!

Gingerbread Cookie Dough:

2 cups all-purpose flour

2 teaspoons ginger

1 teaspoon cinnamon

½ teaspoon nutmeg

¼ teaspoon cloves

¼ teaspoon baking soda

¼ teaspoon salt

½ cup unsalted butter, room temperature

⅓ cup brown sugar

⅓ cup molasses

1 egg

Royal Icing (page 99)

Desired sprinkles or colored sugar

Make the Cookies:

1. Combine the flour, ginger, cinnamon, nutmeg, cloves, baking soda, and salt. Set aside.

2. Beat the butter and brown sugar with an electric mixer until smooth. Add the molasses and egg and mix until combined. Add the dry ingredients and mix until just combined. Divide the dough in 2 and wrap each in plastic wrap. Refrigerate for 1 hour, until firm.

3. Line a baking sheet with parchment paper and preheat the oven to 350°F. Roll the chilled dough out on a floured surface until it is ⅛ inch thick. Using the image below as a guide, make paper templates of each wall and cut out 2 house "fronts," 2 "walls," and 2 "roofs" for each house. Transfer the cookies to your prepared baking sheet.

4. Bake for about 10 minutes, until the edges begin to darken. Transfer the cookies to a wire rack and cool completely.

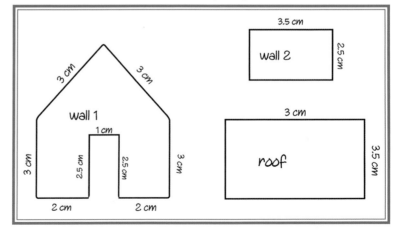

(Continued on next page)

Build the Houses:

1. Decorate the cookies as you like. To make sprinkle- or sugar-covered roofs, pipe your desired design onto the roof with icing and quickly sprinkle sugar on top. Tap the cookie on its edge to remove excess sugar and let dry. If you'd like the entire roof to be coated in sprinkles, pipe an outline around the edges of the cookie. Add a few drops of water to some of the icing, then fill the cookie in. Sprinkle the sugar/sprinkles on top and let the icing dry. Then tap the cookie on its edge to remove any excess sprinkles.

2. Use the thicker icing (not for filling the roof in) to attach the walls and roof. Set the houses aside and let the icing fully harden, about 1 to 2 hours.

3. To serve, place the houses onto the rim of your mug!

GINGERBREAD SKI CHALET TREAT BOX

MAKES 1 HOUSE

This is a fun little centerpiece for any holiday party. Fill it with truffles, candy, or cookies!

1 recipe Gingerbread Cookie Dough
  (page 183)
Royal Icing (page 99)
Brown food coloring
Edible glitter
Chocolates and candies

Bake the Cookie:

1. Line a baking sheet with parchment paper and preheat the oven to 350°F.

2. Roll the Gingerbread Cookie Dough out onto a floured sheet of parchment paper until it is ⅛ inch thick. Use the guide provided to measure and cut out paper templates, and use these as stencils to cut out the pieces of the dough.

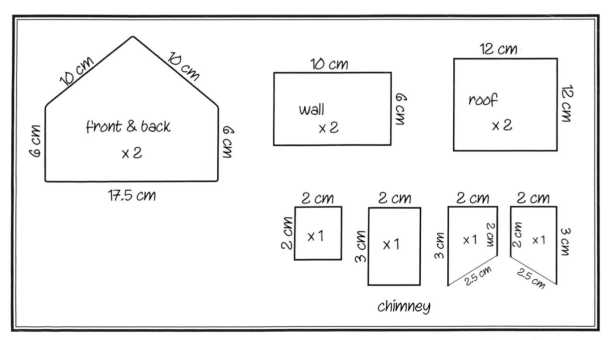

(Continued on page 187)

3. Gently place each wall onto your prepared baking sheet. If necessary, straighten the sides with the side of a knife. Bake for 10 to 12 minutes, until the edges begin to darken. Transfer the cookies, still on the baking sheet, to a wire rack and allow to cool completely.

To Decorate:

1. Dye ⅔ of the icing a light brown color and place both shades of icing in piping bags fitted with #4 (small round) piping tips.

2. Use the white icing to draw the windows, door, and snow onto the walls, roof, and chimney. Add a little bit of water to the white icing and use this thinner icing to fill in the snow on the roof. While the icing is still wet, generously sprinkle some edible glitter on top.

3. Use the brown icing to draw the beams and roof shingles onto the house. Allow the icing to fully set, about 1 hour.

Build the Chalet:

1. Build the chalet using the brown icing as glue. This will result in a cleaner look than white icing. Make sure to only attach one side of the roof. Build the chimney and attach this to the roof using white icing. Allow the icing to set for 1 hour.

2. Place the chalet on a serving tray of your choice and fill it with chocolates and goodies. Attach the remaining roof panel with brown icing and allow it to set for about 20 minutes. To serve, have your guests remove one side of the roof to reveal the treats inside!

Homemade Hot Chocolate
Ornaments, page 207

DRINKS

Classic Hot Chocolate

This is my go-to hot chocolate recipe! It uses chocolate bars instead of cocoa powder, which makes it even richer. For an extra luxurious version, replace 1 cup of milk with cream.

7-ounce good-quality chocolate bar
2 cups milk
Mini marshmallows
¼ cup melted chocolate
Chocolate chunks
Sprinkles

1. Break apart your desired chocolate bar and add it to a small pot with the milk. Set to medium heat and stir until the chocolate bar has fully melted.

2. Pour into 1 to 2 mugs and top with some mini marshmallows and chocolate chunks. Drizzle some melted chocolate on top and garnish with sprinkles. Enjoy!

Eggnog Hot Chocolate

Eggnog is a classic holiday drink, and we're bringing it to another level here! White chocolate is absolutely delicious with eggnog, and I am confident enough to say that this will appeal even to eggnog-haters.

4 cups eggnog
5 ounces white chocolate
1 teaspoon vanilla extract
4 tablespoons rum (or 1–2 teaspoons rum extract)
Whipped cream
Ground nutmeg
Cinnamon stick

1. Pour the eggnog, white chocolate, vanilla extract, and rum into a pot over medium heat. Stir constantly until the white chocolate has fully melted.

2. Pour the hot chocolate into your desired mugs, and top with whipped cream. Sprinkle some nutmeg on top, and decorate with a cinnamon stick!

GINGERBREAD HOT CHOCOLATE

SERVES 1-2

Gingerbread spice is the quintessential Christmas spice, so why not add it to winter's favorite drink? Gingerbread spice pairs fabulously well with milk chocolate. It tastes smooth, creamy, and warm. Pour some into a thermos to enjoy on a chilly winter walk or cuddle up with a mug in front of the fire.

2 cups whipping cream
2 teaspoons Gingerbread Spice Mix (page 147), plus more for dusting, divided
2 tablespoons confectioners' sugar
7-ounce good-quality milk chocolate bar
2 cups milk
Candied ginger pieces
Gingerbread man cookie (page 57)

1. First, make the whipped cream topping. Pour the whipped cream, 1 teaspoon Gingerbread Spice Mix, and confectioners' sugar into a bowl and beat with an electric mixer until stiff peaks form. Place in a piping bag fitted with a #2D (large star/flower) piping tip. Place the piping bag in the fridge while you make the hot chocolate.

2. Break apart the chocolate bar and add it to a small pot with the milk and 1 teaspoon Gingerbread Spice Mix. Set to medium heat and stir until the chocolate bar has fully melted.

3. Pour into 1 or 2 mugs. Top with a swirl of whipped cream and garnish with some candied ginger, Gingerbread Spice Mix, and a gingerbread man cookie.

Reindeer Hot Chocolate

SERVES 1-2

Cute and delicious! Combining two different kinds of chocolate is a great way to enjoy chocolate in a new way. White chocolate adds a lightness to milk chocolate and they are delicious when paired together. The only thing you have to worry about is whether you will eat the gingerbread antlers on the side or dip them into the hot chocolate!

Gingerbread Cookie Dough (page 183)
2 cups whipping cream
2 tablespoons confectioners' sugar
1 teaspoon vanilla extract
1 tablespoon cocoa powder
4 ounces good-quality milk chocolate
4 ounces good-quality white chocolate
2 cups milk
2 red jujubes
Gold sprinkles

Make the Antler Cookies:

1. Roll the Gingerbread Cookie Dough out between 2 sheets of parchment paper until it is ¼-inch thick.

2. Use a sharp knife to draw antlers. Cut a notch 1 inch into the base of each antler, making it 3 times as wide as the rim of your mug. The cookie will expand while baking, which may cause the notch to shrink. You will need 2 antlers per mug.

3. Place the antlers on a baking sheet lined with parchment paper and bake at 350°F for 10 minutes, or until the edges are starting to brown. Cool completely.

Make the Whipped Cream:

1. Place the whipping cream, confectioners' sugar, and vanilla extract in a bowl and beat with an electric mixer until stiff peaks form.

2. Set aside half of the cream. Add the cocoa powder to the remaining cream and beat until combined and stiff peaks form.

3. Spoon both flavors of cream vertically into a piping bag fitted with a #2D (large star/flower) piping tip. Each flavor of cream should vertically take up half of the piping bag.

4. Set the piping bag in the fridge until needed.

Make the Hot Chocolate:

1. Place the milk chocolate and white chocolate into a small pot, along with the milk. Set to medium heat and stir until the chocolate bar has fully melted.

2. Pour into 1 to 2 mugs and top with a swirl of the whipped cream.

3. Stick the antlers onto each mug. Slice a small slit into the bottom of a jujube and stick to the front of the mug. Sprinkle some gold sprinkles on top and enjoy!

Chocolate Almond Hot Chocolate

SERVES 1-2

This delectable hot chocolate is perfect for anybody who is lactose intolerant, as well as any fans of chocolate almonds!

2 cups almond milk, vanilla flavor
2 ounces good-quality milk chocolate

1. Heat the almond milk in a small pot, until hot.

2. Add the milk chocolate and whisk until the chocolate and milk are fully combined.

3. If desired, use a milk frother to froth the hot chocolate. The milk will only froth nicely when mixed with the chocolate, so if you're making a large batch, froth the hot chocolate just before serving.

4. Pour into mugs and enjoy!

PEPPERMINT MOCHA

SERVES 1-2

This delicious mocha uses both milk and dark chocolate, which creates a very smooth, chocolaty flavor. The recipe uses instant coffee, but this can easily be replaced with 1 to 2 shots of espresso if you have an espresso machine at home.

2 cups milk
4 ounces good-quality dark chocolate
4 ounces good-quality milk chocolate
2 sachets instant coffee (approx. 1 teaspoon per sachet)
1 teaspoon peppermint extract
Whipped cream
Festive sprinkles and garnishes

1. Place the milk, dark chocolate, milk chocolate, instant coffee, and peppermint extract in a pot and set to medium heat. Whisk constantly until the chocolate has melted.

2. Pour the hot chocolate into 2 mugs. Top with whipped cream and your desired garnishes. Enjoy!

Red Velvet Santa Hot Chocolate

SERVES 1-2

This delicious hot chocolate is everyone's favorite flavor, and even has a cream cheese rim! It looks just like the fluffy trim on Santa's suit.

Cream Cheese Frosting:
4 ounces cream cheese, room temperature
2 tablespoons confectioners' sugar
1 teaspoon vanilla extract
Edible glitter (optional)

Hot Chocolate:
2 cups milk
2 ounces dark, milk, or white chocolate, finely chopped
Red food coloring

Make the Cream Cheese Frosting:

1. Place the cream cheese, confectioners' sugar, and vanilla extract in a bowl and beat with an electric mixer until smooth.

2. Place the frosting into a piping bag fitted with a #2A (large round) piping tip.

3. Pipe some cream cheese frosting around the edges of your desired mugs and sprinkle some edible glitter on top. Place the mugs in the fridge until you are ready to serve the hot chocolate.

Make the Hot Chocolate:

1. Pour the milk into a small pot and set to medium heat.

2. Add the chocolate and red food coloring and stir until the chocolate has fully melted.

3. Pour the hot chocolate into the mugs and enjoy!

Peanut Butter Hot Chocolate Melts

MAKES ENOUGH FOR 2 SERVINGS OF HOT CHOCOLATE, 4 TREES TOTAL

These sweet little trees are a great party favor or gift idea! Each mug uses one green tree and one marbled tree—package them together in pairs and include a little handwritten note on how to serve. You'll be the gift-giver of the year, guaranteed!

½ cup green candy melts, melted
½ cup good-quality milk chocolate, melted
¼ cup peanut butter

1. Set a pine tree chocolate mold on a flat surface. Coat (but do not fill) the insides of half of the molds with green candy melts. Drizzle the candy melts onto the remaining half of the molds. Fill the drizzled molds with milk chocolate. Place the mold in the freezer until the chocolate has set, about 20 minutes.

2. Place the peanut butter in a piping bag fitted with a round tip. Fill the green chocolate shells with peanut butter and pour more green candy melts on top, sealing the peanut butter inside. Return to the fridge to set, about 20 minutes.

3. Your melts are now done! When you'd like to serve, place a green chocolate melt and a milk chocolate melt into a mug with about 1 cup of hot milk per serving. The marbled tree will create the hot chocolate while the green tree will add the peanut butter flavor! Stir the milk until the trees have fully melted and enjoy your peanut butter hot chocolate!

HOMEMADE HOT CHOCOLATE ORNAMENTS

EACH ORNAMENT MAKES 2 CUPS HOT CHOCOLATE

These ornaments are an adorable idea to add to your own tree, or as gifts for friends this season. When looking for the baubles, I recommend plastic ones with removable silver stoppers. They can be found at big box craft stores during the holidays.

Clear plastic ornaments for filling
¼ cup confectioners' sugar
¼ cup powdered coffee creamer
¼ cup skim milk powder (or coconut milk powder)
2 tablespoons unsweetened cocoa powder
Mini chocolate chips
Festive sprinkles
Mini peanut butter cups
Salted caramel chips
Edible glitter
Mini marshmallow bits

1. Cut the end off a piping bag large enough to fit into the opening of the ornaments. Stick the piping bag into the opening to act as a funnel. First pour the confectioners' sugar into the ornament and jiggle the ornament slightly to flatten the surface. Repeat with the coffee creamer, skim milk powder, and cocoa powder.

2. Add your desired toppings or flavorings:
   For an extra chocolaty hot chocolate, add mini chocolate chips.
   For a festive hot chocolate, add festive sprinkles.
   For peanut butter hot chocolate, add mini peanut butter cups.
   For caramel hot chocolate, add salted caramel chips.
   For coconut hot chocolate, use coconut milk powder instead of skim milk powder and add edible glitter as a garnish.

3. Top with mini marshmallow bits, then seal the ornaments closed. Hook the ornaments onto trees with string.

4. To make the hot chocolate, empty one ornament into a pot and add 2 cups water. Bring the mixture to a simmer, then pour into mugs and enjoy!

Hot Chocolate Charcuterie Board

This time of the year is filled with parties, and this is such a fun way to celebrate! Make your favorite hot chocolate recipe (mine is the Classic Hot Chocolate on page 191) to serve alongside this sweet charcuterie board and invite your guests to flavor and decorate their hot chocolate! Add more or less according to your guests and party size—kids will love lots of options!

3 cups marshmallows
½ cup chocolate kisses
½ cup chewy caramels
½ cup whipped cream
5 rock candy sticks (3 red, 2 green)
½ cup peanut butter chips
¼ cup sweetened coconut shavings
½ cup chocolate curls
¼ cup white chocolate pieces
½ cup mini chocolate peanut butter cups
5 candy canes
1 cup white chocolate pretzels
6 chocolate hazelnut truffles
½ cup ruby chocolate chips
¼ cup crushed candy canes

1. Arrange all your desired ingredients on a large cutting board. You can use small ramekins or dishes to hold some ingredients, which will add depth and visual interest.

2. Serve along some plain hot chocolate (I recommend Classic Hot Chocolate, page 191) and invite your guests to pick their toppings and flavorings!

Acknowledgments

First and foremost, I want to thank *you*—my amazing readers and subscribers! I would not be here today without your unending love and support. I am so humbled that my creations have brought you joy and I am always ecstatic when I see my recipes re-created in your homes. I have been able to become a cookbook author because of your support. Please know how appreciative I am of all of you—every like, comment, and follow warms my heart and makes me want to work even harder for you.

I also want to thank my amazing editor at Skyhorse, Leah Zarra. She has been with me since my first book, *Unicorn Food*, and is one of the kindest, most hardworking people I have ever met. Any ridiculous idea from me, including asking if we can put glitter on a book cover, has been met with such kind-

ness. Thank you so much for believing in me and wanting to work with me again. You have made my dreams come true, and I hope that this book is everything that you hoped it would be.

Thank you to my family and my wonderful boyfriend, who happily took these treats off my hands and who cheered me on during my all-night photo-editing marathons. Your belief in me has carried me through stressful times and kept me going during insecure moments. I am so lucky to have such a wonderful group of people who I can call my family.

Lastly, I want to thank my dog, Paddington, for being the unofficial taste tester of my recipes. For photos taken at a top-down, vertical angle, I had to place my work board on the floor and stand on a chair to get a good photo. Without fail, Paddington made himself available to sneakily lick the edges of cupcakes and tarts while I wasn't looking, which certainly added a sparkle to each shoot.

The beginning of my Candy Cane Cupcake-Cake on page 59!

Index

CONVERSION CHARTS

METRIC AND IMPERIAL CONVERSIONS
(These conversions are rounded for convenience)

Ingredient	Cups/Tablespoons/Teaspoons	Ounces	Grams/Milliliters
Butter	1 cup/16 tablespoons/2 sticks	8 ounces	230 grams
Cheese, shredded	1 cup	4 ounces	110 grams
Cream cheese	1 tablespoon	0.5 ounce	14.5 grams
Cornstarch	1 tablespoon	0.3 ounce	8 grams
Flour, all-purpose	1 cup/1 tablespoon	4.5 ounces/0.3 ounce	125 grams/8 grams
Flour, whole wheat	1 cup	4 ounces	120 grams
Fruit, dried	1 cup	4 ounces	120 grams
Fruits or veggies, chopped	1 cup	5 to 7 ounces	145 to 200 grams
Fruits or veggies, puréed	1 cup	8.5 ounces	245 grams
Honey, maple syrup, or corn syrup	1 tablespoon	0.75 ounce	20 grams
Liquids: cream, milk, water, or juice	1 cup	8 fluid ounces	240 milliliters
Oats	1 cup	5.5 ounces	150 grams
Salt	1 teaspoon	0.2 ounces	6 grams
Spices: cinnamon, cloves, ginger, or nutmeg (ground)	1 teaspoon	0.2 ounce	5 milliliters
Sugar, brown, firmly packed	1 cup	7 ounces	200 grams
Sugar, white	1 cup/1 tablespoon	7 ounces/0.5 ounce	200 grams/12.5 grams
Vanilla extract	1 teaspoon	0.2 ounce	4 grams

OVEN TEMPERATURES

Fahrenheit	Celsius	Gas Mark
225°	110°	¼
250°	120°	½
275°	140°	1
300°	150°	2
325°	160°	3
350°	180°	4
375°	190°	5
400°	200°	6
425°	220°	7
450°	230°	8